The Pink of it

Winning the Battle by Winning One Fight a Day!

Jana Ramos-Ratliff

authorHOUSE®

AuthorHouse™
1663 Liberty Drive
Bloomington, IN 47403
www.authorhouse.com
Phone: 1 (800) 839-8640

Published by AuthorHouse 06/05/2017

ISBN: 978-1-5246-9203-2 (sc)
ISBN: 978-1-5246-9202-5 (e)

Special "Thank You"

I want to say a special "Thank You" to Craig and Chris Villwock, owners of TLC Insurance Group, the company I currently work for and work with. It is a privilege to work for such men of integrity. I am honored to be part of their team.

Craig and Chris, thank you not only for helping me to get this book published as well as your support in other aspects of my life.

WWW.TLCINSURANCEGROUP.COM

Dedicatory

I dedicate this book to all women, men, and children who are directly or indirectly affected by cancer. My wish for you is that your find hope and strength to continue to fight and that you find many positive outcomes for each not so positive experience you have.

Acknowledgments

First and foremost, I want to thank God for my existence and for being here today; for who I am; and for what I have. God has always been part of my life and it wasn't different throughout this treatment. I trusted in Him and I did my part.

Then I want to say thank you to my family, Joe and our son Maximus, and step-daughter Kelsey. They were there for me every day of this journey. They were the ones who saw me every day and helped with all the little and big details of a daily life activities. My gratitude for you is beyond what words can say. Thank you!

Next, I would like to thank my family in Brazil, my mom Aurora who is the most amazing person in this world, the one who taught me everything I know. I am what I am because of her and I am proud to say that. My father Silvio and brothers Junior and his wife Janaina, brother Eric and wife Bianca, and brother Hugo. I know that even with the distance and barriers with the language in reading my blog that was written in English only, I was on your daily thoughts and prayers. Thank you! Also want to say a big thank you to my special American family here, Betty and Jim. Betty was my first English teacher here in America when I was an exchange student back in 2000. Since then, we became close friends and even closer when I moved back here in 2004. During this treatment, Betty was always checking on me and offering her support. Many times, she would come and take Max for a few hours so I could rest. Other times she would just comfort me with her words of wisdom or take me out for lunch. She also fights several battles but is always smiling and willing to help. Thanks Betty! Without the support of these wonderful family members, things would have been very difficult.

I would like to mention here the names of everyone who, in one way or another, touched my life during that time but I am afraid I would be missing someone because I know that there are many people who were cheering and praying for me but not necessarily signed my journal or made any comments. I know that for sure because here and there I bump into someone who tells that they were following my journal and praying for me but I had no idea at that time. But I do want to mention some of them and the special reason why they were essential in this journey: The idea of writing the journal came from my dear friend Sandy R. If it wasn't for you, I wouldn't have started my own journal. Big THANK YOU!

Sandy has always been a dear and close friend, before, during and after the treatment. Sandy, thank you for all your support. You went through very similar situation and your words of comfort helped me during my treatment. ILY (funny thing: she used to put this at the end of texts or comments and I did not know what it meant, until one day it hit me: I Love You!)

I also want to thank caringbridge.com staff who made it easy and fun to write. It's a free website and very friendly user. Thank you, all the staff, and whoever had the idea to create this website.

Mandy Moles, you were very close to me during that time. You think you didn't do much but I know I was on your prayers and thoughts a lot. The breakfasts, lunches, and dinners that you, Sandy, and I often had, meant a lot to me!!

I want to thank the Pink Ribbon Girls – www.pinkribbongirls.org – for the support I received, free meals and free house cleaning. You girls do a wonderful job in helping us! Thank you!

I still want to mention some names here but, they are by no means in order of anything. If I could number them in order of favorites they would all be # 1!

So, I will start with someone who deserves the credit for the name of my book plus she is someone special that was always worried about me: Lorena Hall. She was not only there for me any time I needed her but she also helped naming the book. Yes, "The Pink of It" was her idea and I loved it!! Thank you, Lorena!!! ILY!!

Melanie, Josh, Asenath, and Anna your concerns about my wellbeing were always present every time I heard from you on a text, or a comment on my journal, on our gatherings. Thank you! And thank you Melanie for my wigs!! You definitely know how to cheer me up!

Julie, you were so sweet and your almost daily words of love made a huge difference. I would log in and go straight to see what you had wrote me. So, thank you for taking the time to do that.

Emmie and Silvia, you also followed me with your love, prayers and lots of warm comments to cheer me up. Thank you!

Alison, I know you also followed my journal and I know I have always been on your prayers, before, during and after. Thank you for keeping me close to your heart.

The list could go on and on here. My managers Laura and Becky were amazing in working with me and helping to get through chemo and radiation without losing my job. Thank you!

Trudy Huffman, I lost count of how many cards, chocolates, flowers, etc you sent me. You are so sweet. I am blessed for having you in my life.

Lauri Schwalm, you also followed my journey and helped in any way you could. You, Janet Lee, and Tom Birchfield helped with your prayers and warm thoughts. Thank you!

My friends Katia (in Switzerland) and Mary Lucy and Janete Franca Xavier (in Brazil) I know the three of you were freaking out thinking that you wouldn't see me again, but guess what?? It's not that easy to get rid of me! Hahaha – Te amo amigas!

All the call center staff, and other departments of CareSource, all of my Brazilian friends here and in Brazil, and even the people I never met, I want to thank you for thinking of me during that time.

And lastly but not least, my medical team: Dr. Jeremy Crouch (OBGYN), my breast surgeon and Medical Assistant Karensa, my oncologist and Medical Assistant Amy, my lovely nurse Stacy Lynn! Dr. Rebecca Paessun (Radiation) and the happy and upbeat radiation team! And off course, all their office staff who were always very pleasant and prompt to help with paperwork for FMLA and Disability, scheduling or changing appointments, prescriptions requests, bills, etc… you name it! They do a lot, it's non-stop! Thank you!

I hope you enjoy reading my journey and that it brings hope to you.

Love,
Jana

JANA'S JOURNEY – "THE PINK OF IT"

As my favorite author Matthew Kelly says, life is made of choices.

Every day we have to make decisions: go to work or stay home? black pants or brown skirt? highway or main street?

Every action we take leads us to a different path. The key is to learn how to make the right choices, the kind of choices that will help us become a better version of ourselves. The ones that will help us to get closer to our dreams. The ones that will make a difference in someone's life.

It's never too early to start making the right choices and it's never too late to change your path.

My story is not much different from many other ordinary stories out there.

Throughout my life, I have made many choices. Some of them led me to where I wanted to be to make some of my dreams come true. Others, not so much. But life goes on and we have to continue to make choices and accepting the consequences.

At the age of 35, breast cancer decided to remind me a couple of lessons: We are not invincible and we are not irreplaceable.

Sometimes in life we really need to slow down and think about what matters the most. For me, it's my family, friends, and perhaps the ones who need me but don't necessarily know who I am: volunteer work. It gives me satisfaction to help people I don't know.

Here is a little bit about myself. I was born and raised in Brazil. From my mom's 4 children, I was the only daughter, second to oldest. Also, the only one who left Brazil to adventure life in another country.

I have been living in the USA since 2004. Got married in 2005 and had a son, Maximus, in 2007.

I hope that you enjoy walking this journey with me.

I hope you become a better version of yourself on each decision you make.

Love,

Jana

Diagnosis: Left Breast Cancer Positive
Estrogen Receptor: Negative
Progesterone Receptor: Positive
HER2 protein expression: Negative

Bloom–Richardson Grading score: 3 – which, from what I have been reading, it is stage 1. According to https://community.breastcancer.org/forum/96/topics/770715, they explain that scores 3,4,5 (or stage 1) is the lowest. Well-differentiated breast cells; cells generally appear normal and are not growing rapidly; cancer arranged in small tubules.

Treatments recommended by the doctors:

Doxorubicin (Adriamycin) + Cyclophosphamide (Cytoxan) = 4 sessions, 1 every 21 days.
Taxol= once a week for 12 weeks.
3 weeks break.
6-7 weeks of radiation, once a day, 5 days a week.

How Everything Started

"Life is a succession of moments. To live each one is to succeed." - Corita Kent

Before June 14th, 2013 I had been lucky in terms of health.

Every time I had to update my profile at the doctor's office, you know how you have to mark down your symptoms, health history, surgeries, etc... so, mine is always pretty simple: C-Section on 5/18/07 when I had my wonderful son Maximus and right after that time, was when my migraines started too. Those were the two major health information on my profile. C-Section and Migraines. That's it. Everything else is big scroll down with the pen on the "NO" column.

Well, after June 14th, 2013 things changed a little bit. I am already feeling overwhelmed with so many procedures I have done and how my health history has changed in only 6 months. And this is just the beginning.

Because of that, and a couple of other reasons, I decided to start a journal, so one day I when my memory finally fails on me, I can go back to my journal and tell those doctor's office everything I have had in my life. I admire and appreciate everyone who works in the medical field, starting with the employees of a health insurance call center who have to keep up with all the changes in the healthcare field to the surgeons who operated me. I really do appreciate them all. Every time I enter a hospital I just want to say "thank you" to everyone who works there because it is a very sad place and they still have to keep up the smile in their faces. So, to all health care employees, a big "THANK YOU" from me to you! But the main idea of this journal is to document my treatment and I how I am feeling every day to compare my feelings and maybe somehow help someone else too. Another purpose of this journal is to bring awareness to young ladies out there who are afraid of having their first mammogram. Preventive mammograms are essential in our lives ladies. Don't be afraid, just get it done!

But before I start my daily journal on my treatment, I want to write down how everything started so you have an idea how I discovered my breast cancer and what were the options of treatments I was given.

Love,

Jana

Manuela wrote on Jan 24, 2014 9:39pm: "Jana, estou conhecendo seu blog agora mas pensando em você bastante desde a última vez que nos vimos no meu casamento, que foi tão especial ter sua presença! Estou adorando sua positividade! Te adoro minha amiga!" ("Jana, I am just now finding out about your blog but I have been thinking a lot about you since the last time we saw each other, at my wedding, which was very special to have you there. I love your positivity! I adore you my friend!")

Sandy R. wrote on Jan 7, 2014 8:47pm: "I know exactly what you mean. My health history was relatively event free too, for 56 years until I got the diagnosis. We were both blessed. Still are ultimately. At least that's how I choose to look at it. Attitude is everything! :-) I look forward to reading your blog posts. Sleep well tonight!"

June/14/13 - Preventive Exams - Yearly Checkups - More important than you would imagine!

So, on June 14th, 2013 I went to see my OBGYN, Dr. Jeremy Crouch, for my annual checkup and that's when I asked him to request my first mammogram. He thought it was not necessary but he agreed with me after I explained to him that I had just turned 35 and that my paternal aunt had had breast cancer and that I wanted to start having mammograms every year too. I also worked in a health insurance company and we did a lot of preventive care campaigns on mammograms and that if you had a case in your family, you can start checking as early as when you turn 35. Well, we need to be careful with what we wish for.

July/02/13 - 1st Mammogram - Good Sam North in Englewood

On July 2nd, 2013, I went in for my first mammogram. You know, just a normal exam, in and out of the place with no worries, after all, I am only 35, too young to have anything.

Well, not really. After my first set of pictures, I asked the nurse if she was done and if I could get dressed and for my surprise, she asked me to "hang in there" because she wanted to show my pictures to the doctor and by the way, she also asked that I remained undressed. She said that she was seeing something on the left breast that she did not see it on the right one.

That did not sound good. What happened to "in and out" with no worries?

Life is sure full of surprises.

The nurse comes back out to the waiting room where I was sitting with other ladies also waiting for something. I wondered if they also had to have their pictures shown to the doctor like me. The nurse sends me for an ultrasound on my left breast.

After the ultrasound was done, they tell me that it was just a "little cyst" and that they wanted me to follow up with my doctor but probably nothing was going to happen and asked me to come back in six months.

Aug/26/2013 - Another visit with OBGYN

On August 26th. 2103, I went to talk to Dr. Crouch to talk about my migraines and the possibility of having an IUD. My migraines are mainly around my period and I wanted to try the IUD.

I also asked him to check the "little cyst" on my left breast that, at that time, was more like a lump to me.

He thought it was definitely bigger than just a little cyst and asked if I wanted to be referred to a breast surgeon or wait until my period was over and check again. I chose the latter, after all, I was just too young to have anything serious, right??

Sep/09/2013 - Saw Dr. Crouch again

On Sep 9th 2013 I went back to Dr. Crouch to have my IUD inserted. I guess I decided to ignore the lump and we never talked about it during this visit. I got the Merina IUD and set up another follow up appointment for 30 days later to make sure the IUD was in the right place.

Oct/14/2013 - Follow up on my Merina

On Oct 14th 2013 I saw Dr. Crouch to check on my IUD Merina. Everything was fine.

Also, on this visit I decided to ask him to check the lump on my breast again. At this time, he was concerned with the size and shape of the lump and requested another mammogram and ultrasound for ASAP and referred me to the Breast Surgeon at Good Sam North.

Oct/21/13 - Another Visit to the Breast Center at Good Sam North (GSN)

They did not want to perform another mammogram since I had had one in less than 6 months, so, what they did was another ultrasound. This time, they did not tell me anything. They just told me that the result was going to be sent to my doctor and I should follow up with him.

That was not a good sign. Right then I had a feeling that something was wrong with me.

Oct/22/13 - Confirming my Bad Feelings

Dr. Crouch's office called me and told me that I needed to see a breast surgeon and they set up an appointment with him for me to go over the result of my ultrasound. From here on, everything happened fast. In less than one week, I was meeting with the breast surgeon.

Oct/28/13 - First Visit with Breast Surgeon

He was very nice and explained everything to me and my husband Joe who was there with me.

He explained that the "little cyst" had become a bigger "something" and that if it was really a cyst, he would be able to drain it. If not, he would have to do a biopsy.

So, after a few minutes of explaining both procedures to us, I gave him the "okay" to start with the first procedure which was to try to drain it. Well, in less than 10 seconds that the needle hit the "cyst", he determined that it wasn't going to be possible to continue. I could see it at the computer screen. It looked like the needle was hitting a rock.

He then, changed the instruments and proceeded with the biopsy. He told us that the result would come back no later than in 2 days. This was a Monday morning.

I left his office and went to work. I still didn't know what to think about everything. People were telling me that it wasn't going to be anything serious, others telling me that it was exactly how they found out their breast cancer. My boss telling me that her mom had the same procedure a few hours later than mine, with the same doctor - lots of information to process. But I was still trying to be positive about everything. After all, I am only 35 years old and bad things don't happen to us, right??

Oct/29/13 - The Truth: I Am Not That Young to Have Breast Cancer

The breast surgeon's medical assistant, Karensa, calls me on my cell phone. I am at my desk at work. It was about 3pm. She asked if I had a moment to talk. I told her that I did but I wanted to go in the huddle room.

I thought she was going to tell me that everything was okay because they told me that when the results came back, if it was something serious they would call me back into the office to talk to me but if it was nothing to worry about, they would give me the information over the phone.

Well, I guess I either understood wrong or Breast Cancer is just that normal nowadays. Karensa did not hesitate to tell me over the phone that my result showed "Positive Breast Cancer" and that my next step was to see the breast surgeon either the next day afternoon which was a Wednesday or on Friday Morning, at 9am. Because of Joe's work schedule I opted for the Friday appointment.

I hung up the phone with her and the first person I saw was my manager Laura. I was lost and did not know what to do. How could I have received an information like that over the phone at work? I was so glad I was surrounded by people who love and care about me. They gave me the support I needed at that time.

I also called Joe and my friend Betty to give them the news. And tried to continue my day like if I hadn't received any phone calls in that afternoon. It was not easy but I made it until the end of the day.

I got home and tried to do some research but I did not have enough information about what type of breast cancer I had, how big the lump was, the stage, nothing... all I was reading was general information which was not helping much.

So, I decided that I would call the breast surgeon's office first thing in the morning to request more information over the phone or ask if they still had the Wed appointment available. Waiting until Friday was not going to happen.

Sleeping that night was almost impossible. My mind didn't want to stop thinking about all the changes that was going to happen in my life.

Oct/30/13 - Meeting with the breast surgeon

I called his office first thing in the morning and they informed me that there was a cancellation and asked if I could come in today at 9ish. I immediately said yes.

I am so thankful for having a flexible job. All I had to do was to call my boss and let her know that I was going to be late because I had to talk to my doctor. Not too many places are like that. Thank you, manager Becky, for being so understanding and flexible with me.

Again, the breast surgeon was very kind and patient with me and Joe by explaining everything I needed to know about cancer, the type of my cancer, options for treatments and next steps.

He would even answer questions that I wasn't thinking about because this was so new to me.

Because of my family history of breast cancer, (paternal aunt had breast cancer around the age of 50), the first thing the doctor wanted to have done was a genetic test. The result of this test would help him to determine if I should have a lumpectomy or a mastectomy. The lump was small enough to have a lumpectomy but if I had the cancer in my genes, he was going to recommend the mastectomy. If you want to know more about the difference about these two procedure, please go to the American Cancer Society website www.cancer.org but basically the lumpectomy is the removal of the lump from the breast and the mastectomy is the removal of the breast or breasts.

So, after having the result of the genetic test, the doctor wanted me to have an MRI to make sure nothing had spread out to any other place and to make sure the right side breast really did not show any lumps.

Again, I left his office and went to work. It was hard to concentrate. How to tell my employees, friends and family?

Oct/31/13 - Genetic Test done

Now I cannot waste time. I went to have my genetic test done the very next day. It was a bunch of questions about my relatives and finally a blood work. The result would come back in about 10 business days. This was the longest time I had to wait during this whole process.

Nov/08/13 - Genetic Test Results come back

It was Friday. I was exhausted both emotionally and physically. Emotionally with all the information I was dealing with lately and physically at work.

I knew I needed a day off but I wanted to save my PTO hours because I knew I was going to need them all for when I really needed to take time off. However, I could not make myself go to work on this day. I got up on my normal time, 7am, called my boss and told her that I needed a day off. Again, she was very understanding and told me to just take the day off.

Today was also the day mom was going to go to the American Embassy to try to get a visa to come to visit me. This is her second time trying the visa.

My mom tried to come to America when I was pregnant but her visa was denied. She never tried again. It was too frustrating for her. But now, it was different. She wanted to be here with me during this difficult time of my life, so, she decided to try again. Thanks to my brother Junior and his wife Janaina and brother Eric and his wife Bianca, my mom was able to apply for the visa again and today was going to be her interview at the American Embassy to determine if she was going to be able to come here or not. Thank you brothers and sisters for everything you guys did to make this happen.

Max did not have school on this day. I drove him to the daycare where Joe worked around 9am and went to the Catholic Church St. Luke in Beavercreek. One think I like about the Catholic church is that they are always open for us. And there I stayed for about 3 hours and finally got a phone call from my brother telling me that mom had been granted the visa to come to see me!! This was a dream come true for me. I guess this cancer thing was good for one thing. After almost 3 years, I was going to see my mom again. And even better, she was coming to my house!

While I was at church I also got another important phone call. The genetic test place called me to inform that my test came back negative. This was a very important information as it would determine the treatment the breast surgeon was going to recommend.

After hearing from the genetic test place, I called his office and told them that it was negative and that I needed to have the MRI ASAP. Karensa, the Medical Assistant called me back in a few minutes asking if I could have the MRI done at 3pm of today. I said yes. I guess it was meant for me not to go to work today.

I left the church and went to have lunch with my dear friend Betty. Betty was my first ESL (English as Second Language) teacher back in the year of 2000, when I first came to America. We became close friends and I appreciate all the support she has given me during all phases of my life in America.

MRI was very uncomfortable but not too horrible. The noises were loud and I could barely hear the music they put in. But I survived the 50 minutes of loud pictures of my boobies!

Now is another waiting period. It was a Friday and they said that they would have the results in a couple of business days.

Eric Ramos wrote on Jan 9, 2014 6:43am: "Jana, help our mom to get US visa and taking her to your home was our pleasure!!! We couldn't find another way to help you more... I will do whatever I can to help those I love."

Nov/14/13 - MRI results come back

I received a call from Karensa informing me that the MRI was clear and asking if I could have my procedure (Lumpectomy) done on their next available date: Nov 19th. I said yes. I did not want to wait any longer.

Nov/19/13 The Day of the Surgery

Joe took me to the Hospital (GSN) at 7:30 am. The procedure was set up for 12pm.

Betty came to our house to stay with Max until it was time for him to get on the bus. She then went to the hospital to see me and stay with Joe.

Pastor Steve from Concord United Methodist Church came to see me and so did my friend Janet Lee from the same church.

The procedure went well. I was home around 3pm. Janet and Lauri from church brought me dinner. They were very kind to do that. Dinner was yummy!

Nov/25/13 - Follow up Appointment with breast surgeon

He checked on my incision and everything looked great. I was healing well.

The next step now was for the doctors to have a conference to discuss my case to determine if I need to have radiation or chemotherapy, or both.

This conference happens every Thursday but because next Thursday is Thanksgiving, they will not meet again until Dec 5th. Meanwhile, he wanted me to set up an appointment with the Radiation and Oncologist doctors.

12/29/13 – Port insert surgery

Because I will be having lots of rounds of chemotherapy, I had to have a port inserted on the right side of my chest, close to my shoulders. Dr. Wu did the surgery at Good Samarithan Hospital.

Starting on Treatments

01/06/14 - First treatment - Adriamycin + Cytoxan -

I am nervous and anxious. Joe is with me. The treatment center is inside the oncologist's office. There are about 20 recliners for the patients and other chairs for the ones who are there to give support to their loved ones.

Before the actual chemo drug, they inject 2 types anti-nausea. The whole thing lasted about 3-4 hours. Joe was there for the most part, but it's not really comfortable for his back to just sit there. I was okay with him leaving and coming back to pick me up. I also met my boss' mom, today. Remember when I mentioned that she was having the same type of biopsy I had with the same doctor, on the same day? Yes, she got the same phone call from them too.

During the treatment, I felt normal. It was about 3 hours after the treatment that the sickness started. Not fun, not fun.

01/09/14 - Day 3 after 1ˢᵗ chemo

Thank you for all the messages. It really makes me feel better. :)

Day 3 after first treatment. I was able to sleep some but not much. After a cup of coffee, I felt better but now I am feeling like my friend Sandy had warned me: body ache as if I was getting a bad cold.

Lauri Schwalm wrote on Jan 9, 2014 11:37am: "Jana, so glad you are keeping us in touch with how you are doing. I think of you so often throughout the day and - as well as praying for your complete healing - I pray that the after effects of the treatments are so small you hardly notice them and they go away quickly! Love you. Lauri"

1/10/2014 - Day 4 after 1ˢᵗ chemo

Other than a sinus headache that kept me awake most of the night, I am feeling much better today.

Thank you my friend Amanda for your visit! I loved seeing you and your little belly!! :)

1/11/14 - Day 5 after my 1ˢᵗ chemo

The cold really got me. I wish I was feeling better to enjoy the beautiful day. Thanks for all the prayers and positive thoughts.

Camila Passoni wrote on Jan 12, 2014 10:55am: "Oi Jana! Nao deixe a gripe diminuir seu bom humor ou tirar seu otimismo! Estou torcendo por voce! Beijos, Camila" (Hi Jana, don't lose your sense of humor or your optimistic attitude because of the cold. I am cheering for you! Kisses, Camila)

1/12/14 - Day 6 after my 1ˢᵗ chemo - Thank you for friends visit

Thank you my dear friends who came to visit me today. It made me feel better and with more hopes that one day I will go back to work!!

1/13/14 - Day 7 after my 1ˢᵗ chemo - Another trip to the doctor

I barely slept last night because of the sinus infection. So today went to my PCP (Primary Care Physician) and she gave me some antibiotics. I am already feeling better.

Janet Lee wrote on Jan 13, 2014 6:25pm: "Yea! I'm so glad you went to the dr. and got some relief. Tonight, you'll sleep like a baby, hopefully! Take care."

1/14/14 - Day 8 after 1ˢᵗ chemo - Feijoada Brasileira and peanut butter pie from friends Erica and Vanessa

Spent the day with my mom and had the wonderful surprise from friends Erica and Vanessa who were very kind to bring me dinner: Complete Feijoada and peanut butter pie for dessert! Everything was delicious! Thank you so much for being my friends!

Light sinus headache at the end of the day, other than that feeling great!

By the way, I did not mention, but my mom came to see me with my brother Eric. They arrived right after my surgery in November. He stayed for a week, but she will be staying until end of January.

Eric Ramos wrote on Jan 15, 2014 9:59am: "'UAU... fiquei com vontade de comer feijoada...'" (wow that made me want to eat Feijoada…)

1/15/14 Day 9 after 1st chemo - Let it snow!!

It's snowing again in Ohio, a little dust of a fine snow covers the ground of the less traveled roads. It's actually pretty.

I am feeling better and more inspired today even though the sinus is still bugging me.

Christopher Setser wrote on Jan 16, 2014 8:57am: "Get better, lady! Miss you."

Lorena Hall wrote on Jan 15, 2014 12:22pm: "Looking forward to better weather so I can come see your beautiful face❤"

1/16/14 - Day 10 after 1st chemo - "It is better to light a candle than to curse in the dark." - Eleanor Roosevelt

I finally made it to the Cancer Support Group for my free wig but they were behind on their schedule and I could not wait any longer because I had to come back home to wait for Max.

That's okay because I still have hair. They say that I will start losing my hair after my second treatment which will be on Jan 30th.

I am going back to the Support Group on Jan 27th for the wig and to learn how to knit.

They offer a lot of activities for cancer patients. I am going to take advantage of the time off work and do everything I wanted to do but did not have to time to learn.

My mom leaves in less than a week. I will miss her but I am happy that she gets to go home.

The sinus infection is still bugging me but not too bad.

Be happy! :) Jana

Tom Birchfield wrote on Jan 17, 2014 7:46am: "Jana, glad to hear the positive air in your posts. My wife is quite the knitter also. We should get together some time, you & Teri can knit and Joe and I can rock out to Max playing piano. Thoughts and prayers are with you, and hope to see you back among us soon. Tom"

Lauri Schwalm wrote on Jan 16, 2014 6:25pm: "Hi Jana, so glad to know you are some better with the sinus. I was interested in your comment about learning to knit with the cancer support groups. I learned to knit many years ago as a young bride in England and still enjoy clicking the needles, especially during this kind of weather. If you want a knitting companion, let me know. Elsie Kreider, from Concord Church, is a wonderful knitter. Will talk to you soon about Max's piano lessons. Love and prayers coming your way, Lauri"

Sandy R. wrote on Jan 16, 2014 4:37pm: "I'm glad that you're going to a support group, Jana. I didn't go to one, but my treatment wasn't as arduous and long as yours is going to be. So wise of you to take advantage of the time off, too. I'll put my order in for a handmade muffler for next Christmas. ;-)

I kind of enjoyed being bald & not having to worry about shampooing, combing, & styling my hair. Just lazy, I guess. haha They say that you should get a wig that's much like your natural hair, but I always thought that if I were going to get one, it'd be something very different so I could pretend to be a different person. hehe

Thanks for keeping us informed on here. I want to come see you & your Mama before she leaves. I'll call ya. Love ya, Sandy."

Jana Ratliff wrote on Jan 16, 2014 6:03pm: "Hi Sandy, they also have a group for when we are done with our treatment, not sure if you would be interested in going, but it could be something we could do together, think about it!

I know, I think I will enjoy the bald head too. I am already enjoying the short hair :)

I will get started on your order, it may be ready by Christmas of 2016! love you sis, Jana

1/17/14 - Day 11 after 1ˢᵗ chemo - "Nothing in life is to be feared, it is only to be understood." - Marie Curie

I am feeling much better from the sinus infection.

Today I will stay inside the house playing with Max and helping my mom pack. She leaves on this coming Wednesday.

It is amazing to see how much stuff she acquired in only 2 months! Having my mom here was a dream come true! I will miss her but I am happy to see that she is also excited to go home and share with friends and family her experience in Ohio.

Hope you are having a great day! ☺ Jana

Melanie C. wrote on Jan 17, 2014 4:13pm: "So glad to hear you are feeling better and getting out and about. Not many women get to see what their bald head looks like… maybe you should get a tattoo on it lol. That would be very sexy. Now that you are feeling better we should get together for lunch/brunch/dinner sometime."

Jana Ratliff wrote on Jan 18, 2014 11:19pm

I would love to Melanie!

My mom leaves on Wednesday, we can plan something for after she leaves!

1/18/14 Day 12 after 1ˢᵗ chemo - Monster Trucks show: check

I've always wanted to take Max to the Monster Trucks event at Hara arena. Tonight, I can check that off my list.

I wasn't very impressed but it was fun!

My mom had fun there too. She was very impressed.

I felt great today. I hope I can sleep well now! Boa noite. :)

(me, my mom, and my son at Monster Trucks event)

1/19/14 - Day 13 after 1st chemo - "Nobody, but nobody can make it out here alone." - Maya Angelou

Thank you, friends and family, for your support. But mostly thank you my dear husband Joe for taking care of me.

It's getting close to the date when my mom goes back home. I will miss her immensely. She has been my rock but I understand that she needs go back to her normal life.

I slept well and now I am feeling like re-energized. Will be cleaning up Max's toys today. If anyone knows any organization that could use some boys' toys, still in great condition, let me know. Have a great day! Jana

Lauri Schwalm wrote on Jan 19, 2014 11:57am: "It is so good to know that you are feeling better. Will keep your mother in prayers for safe travel and continue prayers for you, Joe, and Max.

1/20/14 - Day 14 after 1st chemo - "The question is not whether we will die, but how we will live." - Joan Borysenko

Since the day I had the surgery to insert the port (the catheter where I receive the chemo), my right shoulder hasn't been right and today it is extra painful. Not sure what they did during the surgery that messed up my shoulder.

I have an appointment with my oncologist this week. I will probably ask for an x-ray of shoulder if it is hurting by then.

Other than that, I had a great day with mom, husband, son and special dinner with my step-daughter Kelsey.

I started to watch "The Stand" by Steven King, it's interesting!

Hope you all have a great week!

Jana

Sandy R. wrote on Jan 21, 2014 4:10pm: "I loved watching "The Stand." It's very interesting and haunting at times. Think of you every day. ♥"

Emmie Call wrote on Jan 21, 2014 1:49pm: "I hope you enjoy been a Stephen King fan as long as I've been reading "grown up" books. He is one of the few authors I have read that I can read over and over again. Thinking of you! Sending lots of love and healing thoughts."

Lauri Schwalm wrote on Jan 20, 2014 10:24pm: "I hope your shoulder gets better very quickly, Jana. How nice to know that you had such a great day with your family. I know you will treasure these next 2 days with your mother before she lives the country. How wonderful that Joe is taking such good care of you. I am sure that will make it easier for your mom to leave you. My love and prayers, as always, Lauri"

1/21/14 - Day 15 after 1st chemo - "The road to a friend's house is never too long." - Danish proverb

Another snow day without school. Luckily, I am home to watch Max. I feel bad for the parents who have to work when schools and even daycares close because of the weather. If you are a parent who needs help on those days, let me know. Max and I will enjoy the company of other kids too.

I am still coughing a little bit but my shoulder feels better today.

My mom goes home tomorrow. Everything is pretty much packed. I hope the weather does not delay her trip back home.

Stay warm! Love, Jana

1/22/14 - Day 16 after 1st chemo - I wonder if even bald I will still have "bad hair" days??? :) Jana Ramos-Ratliff

I was taking a shower this morning and suddenly I noticed that the bathtub was getting full of water. I looked down and I saw a good amount of hair blocking the drain in the bathtub, more than the usual. I ran my fingers through my hair and a handful of hair came off. I thought to myself: "It's finally happening and that's why I've been having a sensitive scalp for the last two days."

Day 16 after my first treatment: it's time to shave it off.

I think this is the first time I freaked out about this cancer thing. I cried a little bit. When I was done with my shower, I called my mom to come to the bathroom. I could see it in her eyes that she wanted to be strong for me too but it was difficult.

I am kind of glad that today is her last day here, I don't really want her to see me going through this phase. I know I will be okay so there is no need for her to see all this and suffer for no reason.

Now is to pray that her flight is not cancelled due to weather and pray that everything goes well with her trip and that she gets home safely.

I will write some more later. :) Jana

Part 2 - Took mom to the airport this afternoon. She already called me from Chicago and is ready to fly to Brazil. Thank you God for this opportunity to have my mom here with me for 2 months! Our time together was great and I will never forget it!

And I can't thank my brothers and sisters-in-law enough for making this dream come true.

When I got back from the airport, I asked Joe to shave my head. It is now shaved - number 2 - and will probably soon, be zero.

It's been a long day. Going to rest now. Good night! Boa noite!

Jana

Manuela wrote on Jan 24, 2014 10:44pm: "Querida!!! Não foi a toa então que eu estava tão pensativa em você antes de ontem e ontem, que coisa!!

Sua beleza atravessa o físico, que é o que está sendo tratado agora. Ser doce, cuidadosa e carinhosa é a beleza que vejo em você e que não vai embora de jeito nenhum!! Um abraço beeeem apertado em você!" (My dear, it's not a coincidence that I have been thinking about you so much these last two days. Your beauty goes beyond your physical aspect which is what you are being treated for right now. Being sweet, caring, loving, are the beauties I see in you and they will never go away! A very tight hug for you!)

Jana Ratliff wrote on Jan 24, 2014 11:28pm: "Tambem tenho pensado em vc Manu.

Estou pra te ligar pra saber das novidades! Beijos." (I also have been thinking about you Manu. I've been meaning to call you to catch up on what's new! Kisses)

Asenath wrote on Jan 22, 2014 7:32pm: "I miss you Jana!! You are beautiful with or without hair!!"

Eric Ramos wrote on Jan 22, 2014 9:35am: "Jana, visualmente esta é a fase critica do tratamento. Talvez seja a fase que nos damos conta do que estamos lutando. Mas tenho certeza que isso não passa do "visual". Seja forte. Estamos aqui, do outro lado, torcendo e rezando por vc!" (Jana, visually speaking this is the most critical phase of the treatment. That's when we really realize what we are fighting against. But I am sure that this will only be "visual". Be strong, we are here on the other side cheering and praying for you!)

Jana Ratliff wrote on Jan 22, 2014 9:31pm: "Obrigada meu irmao (thank you my brother) and thank you Asenath!! Joe shaved my head this evening. I am doing great, it will grow again!

1/23/14 - Day 17 after 1st chemo - "What lies behind us and what lies ahead of us are tiny matters compared to what lives within us." - Oliver Wendel Holmes

---

My mom arrived safely in Brazil. Thank you for the positive thoughts and prayers for her to have a good flight home.

The house feels empty and I miss her already. It will not be the same but I am happy for her.

I had a follow up with my oncologist, today. Everything is going well. White and red blood counts (WBC and RBC) are within normal and so are the platelets (PLT): WBC: 5.9 (low 3.8 and high 10.8). RBC: 4.47 (low 3.90 and high 5.20) - PLT 381 (low 130, high 400).

Next treatment will be on Jan 30th. :) Jana

1/24/2014 - Day 18 after 1st chemo - "Do not let your life be like a shooting star which lights up the sky for only a brief moment. Let your life be like the sun, which always burns brightly in the heavens." Matthew Kelly

I sure picked the right time of the year to be home! It's been ridiculously cold!

I woke up with my monthly migraine today. I took my migraine pill and by the end of the afternoon I was feeling better.

Max went to a birthday party at the Cincinnati Aquarium this evening. He will be spending the night there with his friends. He was super excited!

I am home alone, Joe is working this evening too. I am kind of lost. Haven't been home alone like this for a long time. Not sure what to do. I guess I will just cuddle up on the couch and watch a chick flick!

1/25/14 - Day 19 after 1st chemo - "We can never get enough of what we don't really need." Matthew Kelly

I haven't felt good like I do today in a long time. I cleaned the entire house and did some laundry.

On the other hand, this cold weather is depressing but I am thankful for having a warm house to keep us safe and warm.

I miss my team and the other call center staff. I get messages from them all the time. I really appreciate it. They are awesome!

I miss my bosses too. I am also thankful for working for such great people. Stay warm friends, Jana

1/26/14 - Day 20 after 1ˢᵗ chemo - "People don't care how much you know until they know how much you care." unknown

Today I thought that I wasn't going to have anything to write on my journal, it was just an ordinary day: I slept in, had my breakfast, watched a TV show, did laundry, watched more TV, cooked dinner and so on.

But it wasn't until a little while ago, when I took my shower, that I cried for the second time this week because of my hair.

I know it's just the hair and it will grow again but when I looked in the mirror and saw that most of it is gone, the tears were inevitable.

Hope everyone has a great week! Jana

Jenna Agee wrote on Jan 28, 2014 1:08pm: "I cried when I read this. It will grow back. As soon as this is over you will see how strong you are and how you inspired others. You're amazing Jana ❤"

Sandy R. wrote on Jan 27, 2014 6:44pm: "Oh Jana :-(I understand. I'm not sure what made your tears fall, but I can share my experience with you. When I got my long hair cut, it was a bit of a shock, but I didn't really cry. It was kind of fun. Then when my hair began falling out, it was such a strange occurrence that I spent most of my time giggling about the phenomenon and at how silly I looked as it was falling out. I was amazed at how much hair I really had. Then one day when I looked in the mirror and realized that my eyebrows and eye lashes were falling out, too, I broke down and wept. I didn't cry because I looked ugly or funny. I cried because it hit me just how devastating chemotherapy was to my body - so devastating that it killed my hair. That's when the seriousness of this dreaded disease and treatment hit home. I'm so sorry that you have to suffer this, but I promise you that, just as the Lord says, this, too, shall pass. I'm here if you ever want to talk. ily

PS: I think you're gorgeous! ☺

1/27/14 - Day 21 after 1ˢᵗ chemo - "I Can-Cer Vive!"

Glad school wasn't delayed today, but I sure could have used to sleep in today. I could not fall asleep last night, that wind was so strong, it kept me awake until past 2 am.

Today I have my appointment for my wig again. I hope I can make it. The last time I went to get it, they were running late and I could not wait.

1/27/14 - Part 2

Had an awesome afternoon at the Support Group: got a new wig and learned the basics of knitting.

But the best part of the afternoon, was to meet my dear friend Melanie C. and get two more wigs!! I will be posting pictures later!

Thanks Melanie C. for meeting up with me, it meant a lot to me!! Hope we get together soon again!!

I miss my team! I need another Team Meeting in my house!!!

Gotta finish my scarf, talk to you tomorrow! :) Jana

Lauri Schwalm wrote on Jan 27, 2014 9:04pm" How great to hear what a terrific day you had. Three wigs?! Does each show a different side to your personality? I look forward to seeing you soon. Love and prayers, Lauri"

Lauri Schwalm wrote on Jan 27, 2014 9:05pm: "For some reason my comments have not been showing up as posted, but I do read your blog each day and pray for you. I am glad this last one posted.

Jana Ratliff|Jan 28, 2014 10:04am

Thanks Lauri and I do see your comments, almost every day you write me some kind words, thank you! I look forward to seeing you today for Max's first piano lesson. :)

1/28/14 – Day 22 after 1ˢᵗ chemo - "When one is busy working or helping someone else, one does not have time to think about one's problems." Jana Ramos-Ratliff

I woke up feeling great, shaved the rest of my hair that was driving me crazy and chatted with some awesome people on my phone.

Max is off school today due to weather conditions. Will do some cleaning now and then play video game with him.

Thank you Asenath for the visit! I really enjoyed seeing you!!

And thank for helping me with new hairs! yes, hairs…plural, because now I have more than one to choose from!!

Thank you for reading my journal. I do appreciate your support. Your comments and kind words do make a difference in my life. It gives me strength and hopes I need to keep going.

Love, Jana

This is me with different wigs ☺

Asenath wrote on Jan 28, 2014 4:26pm: "It was great seeing you too! Love the wigs especially the pink one and it's good to see you in such high spirits. Love ya"

Sandy R. wrote on Jan 28, 2014 3:58pm: 'What fun! Different hairs for different personalities. ;-) Looking so cute!"

Melanie C. wrote on Jan 28, 2014 3:38pm: "look at all these glamorous new looks! Awesome!"

Eric Ramos wrote on Jan 28, 2014 1:52pm: "I didn't know you had shaved the rest of your hair. Send me a photo!"

Lauri Schwalm wrote on Jan 28, 2014 11:38am: "No matter how cold the weather may be you have lots of warm thoughts and loving prayers covering you."

1/29/14 - Day 23 after 1ˢᵗ chemo - "We are held back by fear not by limitation." unknown

Had a nice cup of coffee with my friend Lorena Hall and even got some awesome gifts!!! Lorena, it was great seeing and getting to steal some of your positive energy! Thank you!

Physically, I am feeling great. Emotionally, I am feeling scared and anxious. Tomorrow will be my second chemo treatment. I just don't want to go through all the sickness again, especially because I've heard that it just gets worse. I wish I could just receive the treatment and then put to sleep for the next 3 days and then when I woke up, all the headache and nausea were gone.

Please, pray for me not to get too sick. I can deal with the nausea, but the headache is the worst thing ever.

Hope you have a great weekend!

Love ya all! Jana

Stacy wrote Jan 31, 2014 9:22pm: "Hi there my friend! I'm hoping you're home enjoying Max and hubby! Enjoy your weekend ;)"

Tom Birchfield wrote on Jan 30, 2014 7:59am: "Jana, the hairs are looking great, and your spirit are warming us all even in this cold spell. My prayers are with you during your next treatment, praying that you sleep it off and wake up pink and refreshed."

Emmie Call wrote on Jan 30, 2014 6:02am: "Thinking of you and sending healing thoughts."

1/30/2014 - Day 24 after 1st chemo – The day I get my second treatment.

Here I am at Good Sam North getting ready to receive my second treatment of Adriamycin + Cytoxan.I've been blessed to have been treated by a wonderful nurse. She is patient and caring. It does make a difference when we are treated with love in those difficult times. Thank you RN Stacy for your kindness not only with me but I also see how you interact with all your patients. You make a difference in our lives!

Blood work just came back and numbers are good: white blood cells: 5.8, Red blood cells 4.18 and platelet: 384.I just took one of my migraine pills (sumatriptan) to see if I don't get a headache this time. The drug they use for nausea, Emend, gave me headache last time.

Part2 - It's 7:20pm, I don't even know how to explain how I am feeling but I will try.

I got home from the hospital around 1:30pm. Was feeling fine but tired. I did not sleep well last night, I was too anxious. Had a chicken sandwich and lots of water. Went to lay down. Couldn't really sleep but dozed off for a little bit. My body was feeling heavy, it wasn't dizziness, it was a weird sensation. Around 6ish I noticed that the headache wanted to make its appearance for the evening, so before that happened, I took another one of my migraine pills, which doesn't really make me feel good but usually kills the headache after the side effect is gone.

I decided to get up just a few minutes ago and tried to eat, but all I managed to eat was cheese stick and a cracker. Been drinking lots of water though.

I did feel a little bit of nausea, so I took the anti-nausea pill, this time, I am trying the new pill, Prochlorperazine. The other I took last time, Zofran, gave me more headache and did not help with the nausea.

I am going to try to rest now.

I will talk to you tomorrow. Thank you for all the prayers and positive thoughts. :) Jana

Lauri Schwalm wrote on Jan 30, 2014 11:41am: "I pray you will do very well following this 2nd treatment. Loved all of the new looks with your new wigs. Does Joe or Max have a fave yet?"

Jana Ratliff wrote on Jan 30, 2014 6:20pm "Thanks Lauri. No, they are guys, LOL. All they say is that they all look good! :) It works for me."

1/31/14 - Day 25 after 1st chemo / day 1 after 2nd chemo

I actually slept better than I slept after my first treatment. I think the fact that I took a migraine pain pill before my treatment and another one later in the day, helped to prevent the headache I had last time.

I am also not having as much nausea as I had after my first treatment.

Doing ok so far, not feeling 100% but much better than my first treatment. I hope I continue to feel better.

Thank you for all the prayers and positive thoughts! Jana

Me with the wig I chose and a turban hat I got on Amazon.

Stacy wrote on Jan 31, 2014 9:29pm: "Hi there my friend. I'm hoping you're home enjoying Max and hubby while warm and cozy :) This site is awesome. You look pretty in each hairstyle :) God bless ya!"

Chad B. wrote on Jan 31, 2014 3:49pm: "Keep it up and get better faster!"

Melanie C. wrote on Jan 31, 2014 3:26pm: "Yay! so glad to hear this treatment is going better so far! Love the blonde bob!"

Lauri Schwalm wrote on Jan 31, 2014 2:58pm: "So glad you are doing better after this treatment and hope you continue to feel better every day."

2/1/14 - Day 26 after 1st chemo / day 2 after 2nd chemo

What a day! Everything hurts.

Ok, that's it. Back to bed.

I hope I have a better story for tomorrow! :) Jana

2/2/14 - Day 27 after 1st chemo / day 3 after 2nd chemo

I feel better today from the body ache but I did not sleep well. I had headaches all night long on top of the dry mouth and having to get up to go pee every couple of hours.

The taste in my mouth is worse than the worst hangover taste I ever had. It's hard to explain. It actually does not have any taste. It's like if I had lost my sense of taste. It's awful.

Ok, let me try to write something positive: I do have awesome friends and family that cheer me up every day. Thank you so much. It does make a difference in my recovery to know that you are thinking of me. <3 It gives me hope to keep fighting!

Another positive note: a dear friend of mine, Ana Paula, just had a baby girl. Mom and child are doing well but she did have a C-Section and I know how that is. It will hurt a little bit in the beginning but she will be all right. May God bless her and her little one! Love, Jana

Janet Lee wrote on Feb 2, 2014 5:33pm "Jana, even though I do not write often, please know that I am thinking of you and praying for you. I love reading how you are feeling. Thank you for your kind note although I can't figure out how you managed the surprise! God loves you."

2/3/14 - Day 28 after 1st chemo / day 4 after 2nd chemo

An old Cherokee told his grandson: "My son, there is a battle between two wolves inside us all. One is evil. It is anger, jealousy, greed, and resentment, inferiority, lies and ego. The other is good. It is joy, peace, love, hope, humility, kindness, empathy, and truth."

The boy thought about it, and asked, "Grandfather, which wolf wins?"

The old man quietly replied, "The one you feed."

Feeling better today from the nausea and headache but the taste in my mouth is still indescribable. I am not sure is if that is the reason why I am constantly hungry. I eat, but then an hour later I want to eat again. I think the fact that I don't taste the food makes me want to eat something else. Afff... I don't think I will ever find anything that will cut down my appetite. I just love to eat!! LOL!

Yes, about the fable of the wolves, most of you probably already know it. I've been trying to live by it more than ever.

It is easy in a situation like mine to be negative and blame the world for everything that goes wrong and do nothing about it.

Life is a result of choices we make. I can't change my past. I can just accept where I am and hope that I am making the right choices now so I can have a better future.

If you are in OH, watch the news and stay warm! I hear rumors that we are getting more snow!

If you are not in OH, lucky you! :)

Shanti my friends, Jana

Sandy R. wrote on Feb 3, 2014 7:54pm: "I was out of town for a few days, but, so glad you're feeling some better after your second treatment, Jana banana. :)"

2/4/14 - Day 29 after 1ˢᵗ chemo / day 5 after 2ⁿᵈ chemo

I woke up feeling like I was getting sick with the cold: sore throat, running nose and light headache. And that's how I felt pretty much all day.

I found a letter from our director today and this quote was in it. I thought I would share it with you:

"Flatter me, and I may not believe you. Criticize me, and I may not like you. Ignore me, and I may not forgive you. Encourage me, and I will not forget you!" Willian Arthur Ward

Have a blessed evening. Jana

2/5/14 - Day 30 after 1ˢᵗ chemo / day 6 after 2ⁿᵈ chemo

No school for Max due to snow. Looking at the bright side, I am getting to spend a lot of time with my son and I love it! Filho a mamae te ama. Se algum dia voce ler esse diario e eu nao estiver mais aqui, saiba q foi Deus que me permitiu ficar doente para que eu passe mais tempo com voce! (Son, I love you. If you ever get to read this journal and I am not here anymore, just know that I believe that God wanted to me to spend more time with you and that's why I got sick).

Sinus infection again just like right after my first treatment.

My oncologist will see me tomorrow. Other than that, taste buds are still messed up but it's getting better.

Thank you for prayers and concerns.

love, Jana

2/6/14 - Day 31 after 1st chemo / day 7 after 2nd chemo

Went to see my oncologist today because of my sinus infection. He put me on another antibiotic: Bactrim. I hope this time this sinus infection goes way for good.

Other than that, I am feeling better. The taste in my mouth is not as bad as it was but still not 100%.

Going to cuddle up with Max now and watch one of his TV shows: The Incredible Hulk! Nite, nite, Jana

2/7/14 - Day 32 after 1st chemo / day 8 after 2nd chemo

Feeling much better today! Mouth is still the same though. It feels like when you burn your tongue. Still not keeping me from eating!

Had a talk with my HR today and have some return dates in mind. It will depend on how I am feeling, I can't say much right now but I am very thankful and blessed for the job I have and lucky to have understanding supervisors. Thank you CS!

Going to watch a movie with Max now. Joe is working tonight!

Good night my friends! Jana

2/8/14 - Day 33 after 1st chemo / day 9 after 2nd chemo

I met a someone about 9 years ago. We bonded not only because she was friendly and caring but we also had something else in common: Her daughter is from Brazil too.

We were in touch for a couple of years, the kind of friendship that you sit down for a cup of coffee every other week or so to catch up on life, go to for walking at the park together, come over for birthday celebrations, things like that.

At that time, I was expecting Max and then he was born. She loved seeing him.

But then I moved to a more distant area, got a full-time job and our lives started to disperse.

In the past year or so, I have contacted her twice and they were purposely to ask for favors that I knew she would be the only friend I had that could help me. And she did. But I felt bad about that so I sent her a little note to apologize for contacting her only when I needed her. For my surprise, I got the sweetest email back from her reminding me that people come in our lives at different times and for different reasons like the waves on beach and just because our lives went to different ways and we lost connection for a while it didn't mean that she wasn't my friend anymore. She will always be there for me.

I am the kind of person who likes to keep in touch with everyone I meet. I like to know how they are doing, if there is anything I can do for them, etc... but life does get busy and sometimes we don't have that kind of time.

If you were part of my life at one point or another, for any reason we don't talk often, please know that even though I am not in touch with you anymore, no matter how long time goes by, if you ever need to contact me even if it is just to ask for a favor, I will be here for you.

I believe that the true friendship is to be there for one another with no interest or expect anything back.

I am certain that if a friend only contacts us when they need something and remember that we are the only ones who can help them, it does not mean that they only call us when they need us but it means that we have always been in their thoughts and hearts, otherwise they wouldn't even remember us anymore. That's how I feel about my friends!

I hope my co-workers are enjoying "All Staff" this morning. I wish I could be there to hear all about the changes and the future of the company. And I hope they enjoyed the special video I made for them.

I am feeling better today. Sinus infection is starting to go away. The mouth is a little bit better too.

Hope you have a great Saturday and be careful driving. I've heard that we are getting more snow today.

beijos, Jana

This is the video I made for All Staff meeting:

https://www.youtube.com/watch?v=64WIMRrEn24&t=9s

Jenna Agee wrote on Feb 19, 2014 5:38am: "hi Jana. I miss you so much. I love your hats and your pictures. I love seeing how positive you continue to be and I can't wait to see you in the office bringing that positive light to work every day! -xo"

Emmie Call wrote on Feb 10, 2014 5:45am: "Hi Jana! It was so wonderful to see your smiling face up on the screen at All Staff. I know you were with us :) Keep smiling. Love you!"

2/9/14 - Day 34 after 1ˢᵗ chemo / day 10 after 2ⁿᵈ chemo

"There are so many urgent things in our lives each day, but the most important things are hardly ever urgent. That's why we need to identify them, give them priority and place them at the center of our lives". (Matthew Kelly, "Building Better Families").

Feeling alright today. Still having the sinus/cold symptoms, but not too bad. The mouth gets better every day but still not back to normal.

It snowed today. I am so tired of this weather but I am thankful for having a warm home and everything I need to be happy.

I am watching YouTube video of Pentatonix. Incredible group of musicians! Check them out if you haven't yet, you won't regret it! Boa noite, Jana

Lauri Schwalm wrote on Feb 9, 2014 10:24pm: "So good to know you are feeling better. I will look forward to seeing you and Max on Tuesday. Prayers continue for your improved health and happy heart."

2/10/14 - Day 35 after 1ˢᵗ chemo / day 11 after 2ⁿᵈ chemo

I've been reading this book from Matthew Kelly, "Building Better Families" and in the process of explaining how kids need to spend time with their parents, he writes the story about a 5-year old boy who asks his busy father how much he makes per hour at work. His father says, "about $20." The boy then asks him for $10. The father gets mad at him for asking such a question and for asking for money and sends the child to his bedroom. After an hour of thinking about what he did, he goes to his son's bedroom and gives him the $10.The child then pulls up another $10 from under his pillow and gives the $20 to his father and asks if he could buy an hour of his time.

I almost cry reading this story. We spend time with things that really don't matter but forget to give our children the attention they need.

Since Max was born I have always worked full time and missed spending more time with him. Even when we take vacations to go to Brazil, things get so busy traveling and visiting everybody that we end up not spending quality time together.

Now that I am home, it's been great to help him with homework, make his lunch, play with him, listen to his stories about when he is 18 years old, he is going to change his name to Metal Blast. He is going to make metal, especially metal suits that fly (influence from Ironman). Even his Portuguese has improved because we have been studying Portuguese together!

Today I am feeling much better. The taste in my mouth is almost gone (especially after eating 3 pieces of brownies... yummy!).

Hope you are doing well too. :) Jana

Silvia Llacera wrote on Feb 11, 2014 10:14am: "Time is priceless. Such a simple and beautiful story. Brownies take care of everything, certainly! LOVE YA!" Te amo. De verdade verdadeira. Tamo junto hein guria. Fica com Deus. (Love you. I really mean it. We are together in this ok girl. May God be with you).

Asenath wrote on Feb 10, 2014 8:44pm: "Love this and Ironically I just read that same story of the dad's hourly wage just today...good timing.. love ya..I enjoyed seeing you help Max with his homework when I visited you last…you're a good momma."

2/11/14 - Day 36 after 1ˢᵗ chemo / day 12 after 2ⁿᵈ chemo

I can't believe it's been 36 days already from my first chemo! My hair is almost all gone. I still have a little stubble on top of my head. It's weird when I look in the mirror, it does not look like it's me.

The "Chemo Brain" is happening. I often can't remember simple words or names of people that I know but haven't talked to in a while. And God knows what else I am doing that I don't know, like for example, I found my bag of salad inside of the pantry the other and not inside of the fridge where it should be. Oh well, I will be alright!

Even though today I was feeling physically better, sinus/cold is almost all gone, the taste in my mouth is 98% back to normal, haven't had a headache in a while, for some reason I felt a little down today, just wanted to sleep all day. I guess it's just the cold weather. I probably need some vitamin D.

Going to watch a little bit of the Winter Olympics and bed time.

:) Jana

Sandy R. wrote on Feb 12, 2014 4:44pm: "Ah yes, good ole chemo brain. It can be frustrating if you let it. Don't let it! Just remember, this too shall pass. :) Might as well laugh at it & not take it too seriously. Cold lettuce is over-rated anyway. ;) ily"

Silvia Llacera wrote on Feb 12, 2014 8:29am: "Things are looking great it seems like. Even you. I look at the pic you texted me often. Make a bed under a beam of sunlight for your nap today. This winter is killing everyone.

I found my phone in the fridge, don't be too hard on yourself!

And don't forget the brownies! Brownies solve everything!

Love ya."

2/12/14 - Day 37 after 1ˢᵗ chemo / day 13 after 2ⁿᵈ chemo

Now that I am finally feeling physically better, I am starting to feel emotionally down. It's gotta be PMS. :(

Anyways, today was beautiful day, I even went for a walk to my mail box across the street and came back, LOL!

Max does not have school on Friday. I need to start thinking about something fun to do with him!

Going to watch some Winter Olympic sports now. I think it is fascinating the things these athletes can do in the snow while I can barely watch it falling down the sky from inside my living room! :)
Jana

Sheila Thompson wrote on Feb 13, 2014 2:35pm: "Been thinking about you. You are a strong and special woman with a kind spirit and heart. Prayers and hugs to you each and every day. Know that I am with you in spirit. Sheila"

2/13/14 - Day 38 after 1ˢᵗ chemo / day 14 after 2ⁿᵈ chemo

I just noticed that I forgot to write on my journal yesterday!

Well, I slept most of the day today but in the evening, I got the energy to clean the house and bake cookies for Valentine's Day!

I am definitely feeling physically well again. One more week and I will be strong again for my 3ʳᵈ dose.

Anyone has big plans for tomorrow?

Stay warm, Jana

Melanie C. wrote on Feb 15, 2014 3:31pm: "I threw a onesie decorating party for a friend who is having a baby girl next month, I've never hosted a baby shower type party before but it went pretty well! Your crochet hat looks pretty good! Congratulations on mastering new skills! Thinking of you often."

Silvia Llacera wrote on Feb 14, 2014 1:51pm: "Cookies!!! What kind of cookies? Are you like me and do the break and bake or are you the real deal baker? No big plans for today.

Glad you are feeling good. Whenever you are not so up to par, let me know if you feel like some FaceTime! Luv ya!"

Sheila Thompson wrote on Feb 13, 2014 2:40pm: "Hugs and Prayers for you my beautiful friend!"

2/14/14 - Day 39 after 1ˢᵗ chemo / day 15 after 2ⁿᵈ chemo

Happy Valentine's Day! And let it snow!! Yes, we are getting more snow today. (I have to talk about the snow, first of all because my brothers read my blog in Brazil and second, in a few years, when I am reading this journal, I want to remember how much snow we had in 2014, not that I will ever forget this winter, but I just want to register what the weather was like when I was in treatment). Sorry, snow is not my thing. It's pretty but just not my thing.

Silvia, I do the Duncan Hines and Betty Crocker type of baking. I believe that if these companies invested millions of dollars to come up with the best recipe for a cake/cookie, why should I try to invent one on my own??? Besides, my forte is decoration anyways.

Joe's cookies were Reese cup cookies, uhhmmmm yummy!! Max's cookies were cupcake cookie filled with caramel!!

Joe had to work this evening, so I will be celebrating my V day tomorrow morning because he has to work tomorrow evening again. :) But I got flowers and chocolate this morning! :) :) :)

Had a super lazy day. Finished knitting my scarf and started on a crochet hat for the second time. The first time I tried it was getting too big, I had to un-do everything and start from the beginning again.

Max is going to have an O.D. of video game today. He did not have school, so I let him play. He even played online with his cousin in Brazil. It was super cool!

Time to work some more on this hat. I will post a pic of it when it's done! beijos, Jana

Silvia Llacera wrote on Feb 17, 2014 11:50am: "I've heard of that Betty Crocker lady before, is she the inventor of the crock pot? :S HA!

Asenath wrote on Feb 15, 2014 10:21am: "Happy Valentine's day a day late ....Love you and miss you.. I have been busy with packing while dealing with the cold/sore throat that is going around the office. I want to visit you again soon once I'm feeling better...btw if it makes you feel any better about the "chemo brain" sometimes I go looking for my glasses and the realize they are on my face...crazy but funny to think about....hope you have a great weekend!"

2/15/14 - Day 40 after 1st chemo / day 16 after 2nd chemo

Finished my first crochet hat!! See pic below! Now ready for something more challenging!!

Feeling great today, ready to continue the cleaning!

Later, Jana

2/16/14 - Day 41 after 1st chemo / day 17 after 2nd chemo

I don't know, I think I may go into business, LOL! Finished my second crochet hat. It was for a baby girl. See pic below.

I am feeling well today but I need to get out of the house so, I am getting ready to take Max to watch the Lego Movie.

Later, Jana

Emmie Call wrote on Feb 18, 2014 6:02am: "That is sooo cute!"

Silvia Llacera wrote on Feb 17, 2014 11:51am: "I can be your first customer. :)

How was the movie?"

Jana Ratliff wrote on Feb 17, 2014 8:02pm: "Movie was great! It was more fun than what I expected! I need to buy more yarn and I will start working on your order! :)"

2/17/14 - Day 42 after 1ˢᵗ chemo / day 18 after 2ⁿᵈ chemo

Had a lovely day at a friend's house. Ana Paula, you are a great friend, thank you. Had lots of much-needed "girls talk" and met an inspiring BC survivor, Jane. She gave a beautiful bracelet. Thank you Jane. You helped me today with your positivity.

I am already getting anxious for my third treatment that will happen on this Thursday. I can't wait for this to be over.

I hope everyone had a safe drive home today. The roads were pretty bad around 5ish.

And I hope schools are not canceled tomorrow. :)

Love, Jana

Silvia Llacera wrote on Feb 18, 2014 7:19am: "Girl talk is always good. I always have the best ones with you!!! My car was a covered with a sheet of ice when I got home from work last night, but thank God I made home safely. We got a 2-hour delay... 1 gone, 1 to go. :)"

2/19/14 - Day 44 after 1ˢᵗ chemo / Day 20 after 2ⁿᵈ chemo

Feeling loved today! :)

Went to see my American mother and dear friend Betty, got to help her with her IPad and then we had a yummy lunch at Ruby Tuesday!

Got several texts and messages from loved ones today too. Thank you!

Not looking forward to having my 3ʳᵈ chemo treatment tomorrow though, but it has to be done.

Finishing another hat. I am still practicing. They are not perfect but I guess Max will end up losing them anyways :)

Silvia, sorry but Sandy had already placed an order before yours. I need to get hers done first. But hang in there, it seems like the winter will be lasting for a while this year!! :(

Gotta get back on my hat, this has become an addiction now, LOL. I've got to see the end of it before I go to bed. Later, Jana

Silvia Llacera wrote on Feb 20, 2014 10:02am: "I can wait. I am sure there will always be opportunities to wear it since we live in Ohio... Love you and I am waiting to hear good news from your chemo today. :)"

April Lemaster | Feb 19, 2014 4:42pm

Hi Jana, I wanted to let you know that I have you in my prayers everyday!!! And ya gotta kick this in the booty and the reason why.. You have got to teach me how to ride a motor cycle this summer. LOL.. I am leaning towards a scooter but the guys at work said No No No.. must get the motor cycle...But I pray everyday that you are getting stronger and stronger.. You can do this..

Jenna Agee wrote on Feb 19, 2014 5:44am: "ficar strong. i falta de você e não posso esperar para vê-lo novamente!"

My friend Jenna Agee and her son

Jana Ratliff wrote on Feb 19, 2014: : Awwww…Jenna that is awesome. You are writing in Portuguese. It makes me really happy!!! Thank you!

2/20/14 day 45 after 1st chemo / Day of 3rd treatment

Here I am again at GSN (Good Sam North) getting ready to receive my third dose of my first treatment of chemo: A C (adriamycin and cyclophosphamide).

My favorite nurse, RN Stacy, started at 10:45 by drawing some blood to make sure blood counts are ok then they start on the anti-nausea meds.

I will write some more later.

Got home about 1pm. Feeling ok so far but I know it will hit me in a little bit.

Got beautiful flowers from my co-worker Trudy Huffman, thank you! You are so sweet.

Also finished another hat.

I am going to try to take a nap now.

Below are the pictures I got from Trudy, the Brazilian hat I made for my son and me!

Michel Rossi wrote on Feb 21, 2014 10:04am: "Jana... minha amiga de 10 anos..virtual, mas tão presente ou mais que os de carne e osso. Ultimamente tinha sumido, e quando a chamei hoje me mandou uma foto carequinha...quer me matar de susto mesmo! rss Mas com um coração tão grande e uma alma tão clara, ela preferiu dividir os seus momentos difíceis nesse blog, dando luz, força e esperança a tantos outros que passam por situações semelhantes. Parabéns pela sua coragem, minha amiga! Me orgulho ainda mais de ser seu amigo! Conte comigo. Mesmo!" (Jana...my friend from over 10 years... virtual friend but always so present in my life as the real ones. You had disappeared lately but when I called you today, you sent me a bald picture, you almost gave me a heart attack!! But with a huge heart and bright soul, she preferred to share her difficult moments in journal, giving a light, hopes and strengths to others who are going through the same situation. Congratulations for being so courageous my friend! I am even prouder of being your friend. Count on me for sure!)

Melanie C. wrote on Feb 20, 2014 6:49pm: "You are still beautiful, with or without the hair you look great lady!"

Alison Nosker wrote on Feb 20, 2014 10:57am: "I have prayed for you today and will continue to lift you up dear one! xx,"

Silvia Llacera wrote on Feb 20, 2014 10:16am: "With you in spirit my friend."

2/21/14 - Day 46 after 1st chemo / Day 1 after 3rd chemo

Felt ok for the rest of the evening last night and had a good night of sleep.

I am actually feeling better this time around. No headaches and almost no nausea. What I am doing different this time is that I have been drinking ginger ale, sprite and powerade on top of lots of water. I am also eating more fruits and veggies.

I got a very nice surprise text this morning from a dear friend of mine from Brazil. He was first my customer at the Exchange Student Agency, Then we became virtual friends. We never met in person but he is always there for me when I need him and vice-versa. Thank you Michel for checking on me and for the lovely note you left on my guestbook.

I am feeling well today, so well that I forgot to go back to the hospital for my Neulasta shot today at 1:30pm, LOL. It's a shot that helps to boost my white blood cells.

So I ran there at 4:45pm and luckily an angel, RN Lisa, was able to give me the shot, otherwise I would have to go to Miami Valley hospital on Sat or Sunday. Thank Lisa for being so sweet and going above and beyond your responsibilities to help me.

2/22/14 day 47 after 1st chemo / Day 2 after 3rd chemo

Happy 3rd birthday to my beautiful niece Nicole! I miss her so much!

I spent most of the day in bed. Again, I feel like I was hit by a truck. My body aches from head to toe.

I am going to try to sleep again. Hope you are having a good Saturday. The weather was gorgeous today! Jana :0)

2/23/14 - Day 48 after 1st chemo / Day 3 after 3rd chemo

Still feeling pain in my entire body. I have been taking pain meds such as Hydrocodone and Ibuprofen and have been sleeping most of the day.

Sandy R. wrote on Feb 23, 2014 4:00pm: ":-(Hope it passes soon!"

2/24/14 - Day 49 after 1st chemo / Day 4 after 3rd chemo

Tired, slept all day. Still having nausea but still managed to go out for dinner and was so lucky to see this wonderful lady: Ms. Joyce! I was so happy when I saw you! You made my day! <3

2/25/14 - Day 50 after 1ˢᵗ chemo / Day 5 after 3ʳᵈ chemo

The nausea and the bad taste in my mouth continues.

So, off topic now: Had my Jeep Patriot for sale just to see what happens, and today I showed it to someone who may actually buy it. Bitter sweet. I love my Jeep but it would be nice not have a car payment anymore. He is going to give me the answer tomorrow. Jana :)

2/26/14 - Day 51 after 1ˢᵗ chemo / Day 6 after 3ʳᵈ chemo

Had nausea pretty much all day. Not having the sinus infection this time though.

I think because I was taking cold meds and antibiotic for the sinus infection right after my first two chemos, I had not noticed the nausea. The taste or lack of taste in my mouth is horrible too. I can't wait for this to be over.

Although I am home, I have no energy to do anything. It's Joe's birthday tomorrow and I wanted to be baking and cleaning but I guess I will have to wait until I feel better.

Melanie C. wrote on Feb 27, 2014 5:51pm: "I'm sorry you are feeling so badly! Soon all of this will be behind you. Have strength!"

2/27/14 - Day 52 after 1ˢᵗ chemo / Day 7 after 3ʳᵈ chemo

I know, I haven't been very inspired to write on my journal lately. I just haven't been feeling well. At least with the cold meds, I get that boost for a couple of hours but with the nausea meds, all I get is sleepiness.

Today is Joe's birthday. At least I woke up feeling a little better. He has to work all day, we will be celebrating his birthday on Saturday.

Also on Saturday, my youngest brother, Eric, will be here again!! I am so excited that I am going to see him again. He is going to attend a workshop in Atlanta, GA, next week but decided to come to Dayton to see me for the weekend. I just hope I am feeling more upbeat than how I am feeling today.

I guess this cold weather doesn't help much either. It's freaking cold again.

I hope you all are doing well. :) Jana

2/27/14 - Day 53 after 1ˢᵗ chemo / Day 8 after 3ʳᵈ chemo

So, today is day 8 after 3ʳᵈ chemo and I am starting to feel better.

I am getting ready to receive my brother for the weekend, I am so excited!

We are also having a small party for Joe and his friends tomorrow. I hope I feel well tomorrow.

I am watching a totally chick flick (Bachelorette) and finishing a scarf for a friend!

Hope you all have a great weekend! :) Jana

3/1/14 - Day 54 after 1ˢᵗ chemo / Day 9 after 3ʳᵈ chemo

Had an awesome day! Brother arrived safely, I baked a cake, and had some awesome friends over to celebrate Joe's and cousin Roger's birthday. I even had a few drinks and felt just like old times! Pictures below: birthday cake and my brother and my son playing the piano.

Now it's time to rest so I can do something fun with my brother tomorrow! Have a good night!! Jana

Below is the cake I made for the birthday boys and on the right, my brother Eric and my son playing the piano.

Silvia Llacera wrote on Mar 3, 2014 12:17pm: "Sounds fun! I wanna hear about your fun day with brother!"

3/2/14 - Day 55 after 1st chemo / Day 10 after 3rd chemo

Had an excellent cold day! By the way, it's my father's birthday today. Happy birthday dad!

We went to look at the motorcycles at Competition Accessories, then explore the Ohio Caverns, and ended at Mad River Ski Resort. My brother wanted to try skiing but it was too cold, probably about - 15 C, so instead we went to the restaurant and had a beer. :)

I do want to take Max there on a warmer day so he can try skiing. If anyone has children and would like to join me, please let me know.

We came home and watched "Wolverine." I ended up sleeping before the movie was over. :(I will finish it tomorrow!

good night! :) Jana

3/3/14 - Day 56 after 1st chemo / Day 11 after 3rd chemo

Last day of my brother here. I even let Max miss school today. It's the first time he misses school, it was delayed anyways because of the snow, so I don't think he missed much, especially because he is already almost at a 4th grade level on his reading and math, and he is only on first grade.

We started the day with his favorite place to shop: "Menards!" Yes, he loves going to Menards to buy tools. It's so much cheaper than what he would pay in Brazil.

We then did some more shopping and at the end of the day we took him to Dayton Airport where we had a great time drinking Shock Top while waiting for his flight.

I am finishing watching Wolverine now.

Overall, I feel great! There's a little bit left of the bad taste in my mouth, but not too bad now.

Good night, Jana

Me and my family

Silvia Llacera wrote on Mar 4, 2014 7:38am: "Wonderful that you feel better. I am the one sick today, started yesterday.

I bet you are super happy to have seen your brother. Did he buy a bunch of electronics too?

Have a beautiful day my friend!"

Jana Ratliff wrote on Mar 4, 2014 9:22pm: "Silvia, finished your hat! You need to come and get it now, LOL! :)

My brother did not buy electronics this time. He bought a bunch of clothes for his adorable daughter and tools for his wood workshop. He is in Atlanta now attending a conference. He bought electronics a couple of years ago when we went to NYC.

3/4/14 - Day 57 after 1ˢᵗ chemo / Day 12 after 3ʳᵈ chemo

Almost 2 months after my first chemo and 12 days after chemo # 3. Feeling normal today, like if I were not on treatment.

Cleaned the whole house with husband, finished a scarf for Sandy and a hat for Silvia!

It's getting close to my next treatment, which will be on 3/13. This will be the last dose of these two drugs, then I will go on another treatment: 1 every week for 12 weeks. Then 7 weeks of radiation, 5 days a week.

I am going back to work sometime after this first phase of treatment is over. I am excited and nervous at the same time.

I miss everyone but it is also nice being able to stay home and raise my son. His Portuguese has improved a lot! I love to help him with his homework (not that he needs any help). I know I will miss spending time with him!

I forgot to mention that the deal with my car did not go through. Part of me was kind of happy, I really like my car!

Well, it's time to go to bed. It will be another long day tomorrow. :) Jana

Percio wrote on Mar 5, 2014 9:56am: "Bom saber que esta' indo tudo otimo! Bom saber que o Max esta' aprimorando o Portugues dele tambem. A Vivi vai precisar de um amiguinho pra trocar umas ideias em Portugues. :) Beijos! (It's good to know that every is going well. Also good to know that Max's Portuguese is getting better. Vivi will need a little friend to chat in Portuguese! Kisses!)

Silvia Llacera wrote on Mar 5, 2014 7:49am: "WOOHOO! I love my hat, but I love more that you are feeling well! Pray that I feel well this weekend too so that I can go see you! I am going to the Little Clinic inside Kroger today, hoping to get a ZPack, whatever it is it's going around. Everyone seems to be sick. Take good care of yourself.

Will you teach Bia and I to knit? Love ya!"

3/5/14 - Day 58 after 1st chemo / Day 13 after 3rd chemo

Had a relaxed day. Stayed home all day, finished another hat!! Spent time with Max and watched a couple of chick flicks! I think I am getting used to staying inside the house but I sure could use a little bit of sunshine.

Physically feeling great! Mentally, starting to stress about going back to work in about a month. Not sure if I will be ready.

Off to bed, have a good night! :) Jana

3/6/14 - Day 59 after 1st chemo / Day 14 after 3rd chemo

Had my follow up with my oncologist today. He is a lovely doctor. So patient and caring. I love his staff too. I couldn't be in better hands!

I am doing well according to him... well, according to me too. I can't complaint. On days like today, that I drive, go to stores, do groceries, make dinner, bake, clean... I feel like I am not on treatment. I do feel tired though but probably because I spend days not doing much then when I feel better I want to do everything!

And talking about baking, here are some of the yummys I baked tonight! Chocolate cake filled with strawberry and covered with Ganache. And Reese's cupcakes. :) Jana

Silvia Llacera wrote on Mar 7, 2014 9:18am: "It is a great thing when you like and trust your doctor. The family doctor I had here moved out of state, and I can't find one I like now.

Glad you are feeling wonderful! CAAAAAAAAAAAAAAAAKE!"

3/7/14 - Day 60 after 1ˢᵗ chemo / Day 15 after 3ʳᵈ chemo

Had an awesome day with my dear friend Mandy Moles! We had lunch at Olive Garden and then went shopping. Happy Birthday to you Mandy, hope you enjoyed the rest of your day!

I think I am addicted to crocheting. I finished another hat, finally one for me. Picture below.

I was looking at my picture with the new hat and started to think: What the hell? I will be 36 years old this month and I am making pink hat with flowers for me! Do we ever grow up?? LOL!

There's a famous Brazilian song "Pais e Filhos" (Parents and Children) by a group called "Legiao Urbana that says; "...You blame your parents for everything, this is absurd - They are children like you - What will you be when you grow up?" That is so true. We, adults, have responsibilities, well some of us, and we learn with our mistakes, well some of us again... but grow up? who wants to lose the child that still exists inside of us?

I was painting Valentine's Day cards with Max the other day and I told him to use his imagination like I was doing. His answer was: "I didn't know adults had imagination too!"

With all the problems (that we create for ourselves) and responsibilities that come along with the power that we all want to have, it's hard to stop and use our imagination because what we have to deal with in life, is real.

But what if the real is nothing more than our own "grown-up imagination?" What if the problems, power, responsibilities that the grown-ups "think" they have, are nothing more than just their own "grown-up imagination?"

From now on that's how I am going to think: everything is just my imagination. I don't really have any problems, neither power nor responsibilities. My imagination will only be about a perfect life, full of happiness. No more spending time thinking about problems and responsibilities. Time will be spent in thinking about solutions and ways to better myself so I can help others! Let's see how my life will be impacted with this change.

I know this will be a challenge. I invite you to try this with me. I will register here how I am doing and I would love to hear from you how you are doing!

Sweet Dreams, Jana

Me and my pink hat!!

Josh wrote on Mar 8, 2014 10:59am: "I like your upbeat, can-do attitude. Ya got moxie! :) It was very nice seeing you the other day. Thanks again for inviting me to Joe's party. I had a lot of fun!"

Jana Ratliff wrote on Mar 8, 2014 4:41pm: "Thanks Josh! It was nice seeing you too! Hope we can get together again some time soon!"

3/8/14 - Day 61 after 1st chemo / Day 16 after 3rd chemo

Happy International Women's Day!

Having a relaxed day. Watched "Life of Pi" in the morning, cooked lunch/dinner in the afternoon, took a nap, and now Max has a play date so I will probably start another crochet project. Not sure yet what I am going to try today. Need to watch some YouTube videos and see what sounds appealing and easy! :)

So far so good with my "positive imagination" attitude. I actually had a situation today that I had to use it and I hope I am on the right path.

Have a great weekend everyone! beijos. Jana

3/9/14 - Day 62 after 1ˢᵗ chemo / Day 17 after 3ʳᵈ chemo

Goodbye weekend! Tomorrow everything starts all over again. A new day, a new opportunity to make our dreams come true.

Had a great time this morning with special friends Melanie C. and Bill, Josh, and my dear son Max. We went to Frisch's Big Boy for breakfast and I had a delicious veggie omelet. I am doing lent for the first time in my life. I am not eating red meat and chicken. I am going to eat fish on Fridays only. So far so good.

In the afternoon, we took Ruby to the dog park - Bark Park - she loved it! I am going to start taking her there more often. It is so nice to see her running and playing with other dogs!

Finished another hat. A white one. It will be for me too.

Going to watch "Sky Fall" now.

Hope everyone has a great week! beijos. Jana

3/10/14 - Day 63 after 1ˢᵗ chemo / Day 18 after 3ʳᵈ chemo

Feeling well. Had a delicious lunch at a Mexican restaurant with two lovely ladies: Mrs. Betty and Mrs. Marylin.

Spent the evening with my family. My step-daughter Kelsey came to visit us too! Thanks for the visit Kels!

3/11/14 - Day 64 after 1ˢᵗ chemo / Day 19 after 3ʳᵈ chemo

Had another wonderful day! Feeling great! The day was just gorgeous today!

I took my dog Ruby for a walk with my husband in the afternoon and had a special dinner at a friend's house in the evening. Thank you, Eli, for your yummy homemade pizzas!!

Now I am getting Max ready to go to bed.

:) Jana

Asenath wrote on Mar 12, 2014 6:38am: "Glad you were able to enjoy the sunshine.. miss you bunches!!"

3/12/14 - Day 65 after 1st chemo / Day 20 after 3rd chemo

Feeling anxious. Tomorrow is the last treatment of this first round of these two strong drugs. Then, in three weeks, I will start on Taxol once a week, for 12 weeks. Then radiation for 7 weeks, every day.

It snowed and it got cold again today. I've been coughing and sneezing. I just hope I don't get a cold now.

I am going to try to go to bed earlier today so I can get some sleep.

Hope everyone has a great Thursday! :) Jana

3/13/14 day 66 after 1st chemo / Day of 4th chemo

Here I am again at Good Sam North for my 4th and last chemo treatment for this first set of drugs. I could not sleep last night. I think I was too anxious for this last treatment. Hopefully it will go smooth like last time.

I got home around 12:30pm and It's 9pm now. I tried to sleep in the afternoon but it didn't work so well. I am having a different side effect this time. Earlier today I felt kind of dizzy and heavy-body feeling that was even hard to walk. Having to go pee every 20 minutes doesn't help much when you are trying to sleep either.

I ate well - husband made yummy gnocchi and then I had my favorite ice cream: Girl Scouts Samoas from Breyers.

Now the heavy-body feeling is gone but I am still a little dizzy. I tried to sleep again but no success. I guess at this point it is better to wait so I can sleep better all night.

good night! Jana

3/14/14 day 67 after 1st chemo / Day 1 after 4th chemo

I slept fairly well after watching a hilarious and inspiring movie last night: The Internship. The two goofy actors Vince Vaughn and Owen Wilson got the chance to be internists at Google. Very funny and good message on diversity and team work! Check it out if you haven't yet!

Spent most of the day in bed feeling very sleepy and tired. Got up only to shower and go get my shot of Neulasta, the medication I have to have after each treatment to help me to increase my white blood cells.

Joe went to work. I will be hanging out with my favorite person in this world, my son Maximus, until it's time to go to bed again.

Hope you got to enjoy at least a little bit of another beautiful day! 54F or 11C – beijos, Jana

3/15/14 day 68 after 1ˢᵗ chemo / Day 2 after 4ᵗʰ chemo

It's easy to be positive when everything is going just the way you expect.

Hard it is to keep it up when everything goes wrong.

The same goes to being nice to people. It is easy to be nice to the ones who are nice to us. What about being nice to someone who always treat you bad? Who can truly say that you are capable of doing that? I know I am not, but I am working on it.

Feeling like got hit by a truck today. Body aches again, the same symptom from the other 3 times. I know it's going to go away but until then, I just need to relax and try to rest.

Hope you are having a great Saturday! XOXO, Jana

3/16/14 day 69 after 1ˢᵗ chemo / Day 3 after 4ᵗʰ chemo

Okay, I am going to try not to be negative but just don't have any other way to explain how I felt last night and throughout the night until middle of the day today other than say that it was the worse night/day of this treatment so far.

My body ached from head to toe. It hurt to move around on my bed. Everything hurt.

I had to take one of my migraines pills this morning after taking other pain pills. But I am feeling better now (6:35pm) and hopefully will have a good night of sleep!

I know that the body ache will go away soon but this horrible taste in my mouth will stay for a good week or so. Nothing much I can do about it, just hurry up and wait.

I want to thank you my friend Betty for keeping Max busy for me during this difficult time of my life and my husband Joe for all his support.

Will try to watch a movie now.

Later, Jana

Matt Becker wrote on Mar 16, 2014 10:13pm: "Hi Jana! I just wanted you to know that I'm thinking about you. I applaud you for your positive energy and refusal to let cancer beat you. I look forward to seeing your smile at work in the near future.

Sending you positive thoughts!"

Melanie C. wrote on Mar 16, 2014 8:05pm: "Take heart in the knowledge that this is the last time you will have to feel badly from the chemo. This part of your journey is almost over!"

Jana Ratliff wrote on Mar 17, 2014 8:14am: "Thanks Matt and Melanie C.! Yes, I am very glad that I finished this first phase! Melanie, I also finished your hat last night!!!! 👒"

3/17/14 day 70 after 1ˢᵗ chemo / day 4 after 4ᵗʰ chemo

Happy St. Patrick's Day!

Today I am feeling like the day after St. Pat's day some years ago: nauseous and hangover taste in my mouth. I can't wait to feel this way again but actually having enjoyed the holiday!

Time, all it takes is time. Time that we value so much and then when we actually have a lot of it, we don't know what to do. But I will patiently wait for the time when I will complaint that I don't have time for anything because that will be time that I will actually be living my life to the fullest. Until that time comes, I will enjoy the time that I have now to do what I wanted to do when I didn't have time: Rest and pray for better days to come, for me and for you.

I was reading my guestbook and other comments and I just want to thank you from the bottom of my heart for taking the time to send me positive thoughts and prayers. It does make a difference in my life.

When this is over, I want to celebrate my life with each one of you. I think I see a big party in the near future!

Today I got a confirmation of my return date to work: 4/14. I pray to God I am well recovered to go back to the craziness of that call center that is full of smart people with tender hearts and passion to help others and improve their lives.

I was also informed that I will be getting a new team. My former team was given to another Team Leader. To my Jana's Gems, you will always be a gem, no matter where you go. It was a pleasure working with you even if it was a for a short time.

To my new team: I can't wait to start working with you!!

And I just want to register here that today would have been my father-in-law's 76th birthday. A man, a father, a grandpa, with a big heart that I had the pleasure to know and love. Larry, wherever you are, know that we will always remember you with a smile on our faces because you knew better than anyone else how to make people smile no matter how bad the situation was. Max and I will keep you in our memories until the day we can see you again. <3

Nap time. Beijos, Jana

3/18/14 day 71 after 1st chemo / Day 5 after 4th chemo

Had a great day today but now feeling sick again.

Got to have lunch with my beautiful step-daughter Kelsey, today she turns 21! WooHoo!!

And received the visit of an amazing friend from work, Andrea Long. She brought her smile, positive energy and a beautiful book full of pictures and warm thoughts from my call center friends. Thank you so much Andrea for putting that together, you are very special and I am lucky to call you my friend!

Going to finish a movie with Max then bed time. :) Jana

3/19/14 day 72 after 1st chemo / Day 6 after 4th chemo

Despite my uncomfortable nausea symptoms that insist in staying with me, today I laughed like I was a child again. I spent almost 3 hours of Facetime with my best friend Katia. We grew up together and I am sure she knows me better than I know myself. It was the perfect therapy for the kind of day I was having. Mercy my dear friend for sharing unforgettable memories and for creating new ones with me today.

Will hang out with Max tonight and hope I feel better. :) Jana

Katia Seeger Kubler wrote on Mar 20, 2014 1:44pm: "Obrigada vc de me fazer chorar ao ler esta mensagem.... mesmo não sabendo se consegui compreender tudo q esta escrito. Eu te amo minha amiga." (Thank you for making me cry when I read your journal…even though I am not sure I understood everything you wrote. I love you my friend.)

Jana Ratliff wrote on Mar 20, 2014 10:33pm: "hhahha pelo menos vc entendeu q eu falei de voce! Vamos fazer mais marcas de rido nas nossas lindas faces!! te amo amiga! Beijos! (LOL, at least you know I was talking about you. Let's put more wrinkles of laughter on our beautiful faces!!! Love you tooI! Beijos!)

Katia Seeger Kubler wrote on Mar 20, 2014 1:59pm: "Ahh, rido existe sim.... Olha a conjugação do verbo rir. .... http://www.conjugacao. com.br/verbo-rir/nós tínhamos rido.... Bjs amiga" (LOL, "rido" does exist. Look at this website to learn how you conjugate the verb "rir" (laugh)). ***Katia is my best friend growing up in Brazil. We have known each other since we were about 4. I was lucky enough to have many amazing friends growing up, but she lived right across my house and we just spent a lot of time together. Nowadays she lives in Switzerland where she is married with 2 beautiful sons. Because we both left our countries about the same time, sometimes when we talk, we forget certain words in Portuguese or how to apply the correct form of a verb, so, we just make up words and then we laugh at each other. It is the best therapy for when I am not feeling well. Thanks Ka for always being there for me. <3

3/20/14 day 73 after 1ˢᵗ chemo / Day 7 after 4ᵗʰ chemo

I was still feeling pretty bad in the morning. After Max left for school, I went back to bed and slept until past noon. The nausea was still bugging me.

Felt better in the afternoon, although the dry mouth and bad taste are still strong symptoms on this day 7. I guess, just like the other treatments, it will be about 10 or 11 that it will go away.

Had a fun evening decorating a cake with Max, well, I let him do the art. Check out the picture bellow.

Looking forward to this weekend. Hoping to see some special friends, right Silvia?? xoxo, Jana

My son Maximus and his cake!

Silvia Llacera wrote on Mar 21, 2014 7:31am: "Right Jana!!! I can't wait to see you. I am so excited to finally feel better and not be afraid to give you my cooties!"

3/21/14 day 74 after 1st chemo / day 8 after 4th chemo

It was a beautiful day today. I even had a little bit of energy to get out for a few minutes and go to the store.

The taste in mouth is still horrible. I am still doing the mouthwash with water, salt and baking soda but nothing seems to help.

Also, had a little bit of nausea today too. I am hoping that by Sunday, I will be feeling better. :) Jana

3/22/14 day 75 after 1ˢᵗ chemo / day 9 after 4ᵗʰ chemo

What a wonderful day! Don't remember having this much energy in a long time!

Cleaned the whole house and had the visit of my ilustre convidada (special guest) Silvia Llacera and her son Josh, who ended up staying for the night to play with Max! Obrigada guria pela visita, adorei! (thanks girl for your visit, I loved it!) :) Jana

Silvia Llacera wrote on Mar 24, 2014 11:12am: "Eu tambem!!! E agora que os meninos viraram irmaos, temos que fazer as visitas mais frequentes! Te amo e obrigada por tudo! Vc esta linda!" (I loved it too!!! And now that the boys are like brothers, we have to visit more often! I love you and thank you for everything. You are beautiful!)

03/23/14 day 76 after 1ˢᵗ chemo / Day 10 after 4ᵗʰ chemo

Had a great day. Took Max and Josh to go Skateworld and we had fun.

Nausea is gone, bud tastes not 100% back to normal yet. I will get there!

Silvia Llacera wrote on Mar 25, 2014 9:58am: "Josh loved it so much! Thanks for helping our boys become good friends too!!!"

Melanie C. wrote on Mar 25, 2014 6:31pm: "Next time you go to skate world I want to go!"

Jana Ratliff wrote on Mar 26, 2014 7:51pm: "I almost called you Melanie C.! I will next time for sure!!"

3/24/14 day 77 after 1ˢᵗ chemo / day 11 after 4ᵗʰ chemo

Had another great day! Physically speaking, I am doing well. Taste buds are almost back to normal.

Also, had a visit of a great friend from work, Tania M. Thank you for visiting me. It was great to chat with you! Not sure if I am excited to go back to work or if I should try to extend my leave! I'd better stop here... LOL... :) Jana

Melanie C. wrote on Mar 25, 2014 6:33pm: "Everyone at work misses you. Take the time you need to heal, but know that we are SO happy to have you back whenever you are ready! :)"

3/25/14 day 78 after 1ˢᵗ chemo / day 12 after 4ᵗʰ chemo

What a lovely winter we are having this spring! It's 30F and snow again! However, my spring allergy already started!

Overall, I am feeling well today. Day 12 and the taste in my mouth is still not 100% back yet. I think I need a beer to help... maybe by the weekend I will have one! :) Jana

Silvia Llacera wrote on Mar 27, 2014 9:56am: "We need to live in the US for Summer and in Brasil for Summer... Beer? How about some wine?"

3/27/14 day 80 after 1ˢᵗ chemo / day 14 after 4ᵗʰ chemo

Saw my oncologist this morning. He is so kind for such a busy doctor. I am thankful for having him as my oncologist. Amy, his Medical Assistant is so nice too.

But while I was in the waiting room, I was observing the people there. The reception area is big and there's always a lot of people there waiting: some to be seen by their oncologists for the first time, others to follow up after a treatment, there's also the ones waiting to receive their chemo treatment for the first time, or last. They are always so busy!

Each one of those patients have their own story but we all meet in the same place for the same purpose: to fight the battle. Men, women, young, elderly, happy, sad, with their loved ones, or alone, on wheel chairs or on oxygen tanks, African American, Caucasian, Hispanic, Asian... different financial backgrounds, but we are all together just hoping for better days. There, we don't care who has the biggest house or the more expensive car. All we want is to be cured and that we will never have to go through this again.

We look at each other's eyes and smile. It's like we are reading each other's mind. We know how we feel, we understand each other without speaking a word.

Yes, the technology is advanced and the treatments and medicines are much better than what they used to be, but Cancer is still a mystery that not even the most intelligent doctors and scientists have all the answers.

Some people believe that there is a cure but it's not financially interesting for the pharmaceutical industry to present it. I don't know, but if this is true, we really live in sick world. But everything is possible.

I just hope that one day, in another dimension, I will understand why I am having to go through this and that all the pieces of this big puzzle called LIFE will come together. Until then, I will keep trying to become a better person every day of my life by making the right choice for the options that life gives me.

Have a great day! Jana

Karen Beaty wrote on Mar 28, 2014 1:35pm: "Oh Jana, just reminded today to check on you, and I'm glad to read such an inspiring post. The cancer "community" was not the one you picked to be in, but none the less, there you are amongst so many others with the same questions. You are there for a reason, and someday you will know why.

Please give my love to Max, a warm hello to Joe, and a great big HUG to you from me this day.

I will continue to pray for you each day.

With love!

Tom Birchfield wrote on Mar 27, 2014 2:47pm: "Jana, you are putting the puzzle together with your journals, and you know God will help with the final pieces that will help give you meaning in your life. My prayers are with you on this journey, and I look forward to seeing you soon. Today's entry is very heart warming and sincere. Give Max a hug for me and say rock on to Joe for me!

Silvia Llacera wrote on Mar 27, 2014 7:37pm: "Agree with Tom. Today's entry is very heartwarming. God knows Jana, and He cares for you and of you. Even if you don't have all the answers, know that you are loved by many. Keep the faith and the fight. I love you bunches."

Jana Ratliff wrote on Mar 27, 2014 6:22pm: "Thanks Tom, Mrs. Beaty and Silvia. I do hope one day I will have answers for my questions! Tom, we will be going back to Concord church when we are ready. Thanks for your prayers!"

3/28/14 day 81 after 1st chemo / day 15 after 4th chemo

Max was up all night last night with either food poising (we ate shrimp for dinner) or stomach flu.

I started having stomach ache around noon. We went for a walk at Charleston Falls with some friends and when I got home, it got really bad. I was up most of the night. I am feeling better now but will take it easy (it's Saturday 3/29 @ 10:30 am now). Hope it does not come back.

Hope everyone has a great weekend! And Go Flyers! :) Jana

3/29/14 day 82 after 1st chemo / day 16 after 4th chemo

Another cold and snowy day. Glad we are going to KY for a couple of days, it's always warmer there.

Feeling better from my stomach flu but still feeling weak and have a little bit of headache.

I was sad that UD (University of Dayton) did not win. I am not much of a sports fan but I am happy to see that they made it that far.

Getting ready to go to bed now. Have a good night every one! :) Jana

3/30/14 Day 83 after 1st chemo / Day 17 after 4th chemo

We traveled to Monticello, KY today to visit our lovely aunt Emma and uncle Charlie. I drove for about 2 hours and felt very tired. Joe drove the rest of the way.

My taste buds are still not back to normal. I wonder if it will ever be. I guess many things will never be the same, I will just have to get used to it.

Hope everyone has a great week at work, at home, or on vacation enjoying spring break! :) Jana

3/31/14 Day 84 after 1st chemo / Day 18 after 4th chemo

It's been a very emotional day: PMS, my 36th birthday, and I lost my dear uncle Sidnei this morning. He was my father's brother. Even though he lived in Brazil, I was very close to him. When growing up, we used to have long talks. He was the one who got me my first real job at one of his friend's construction company. I worked at the reception desk. I have so many other memories of him that is hard to describe now as the tears run down my eyes.

He left a wife (aunt Gracinha), two beautiful daughters (Renata and Sabrina) and a granddaughter (Julia) that was just born not too long ago. Aunt Gracinha and cousins Renata and Sabrina, I am so sorry about your loss, your husband and father was a great man and will be missed by many people. I wish I was there with you during this difficult time of your lives.

Aside of that event, here in Monticello, KY, aunt Emma is making sure I am having a great birthday: special dinner after a wonderful pedicure, then cake and ice cream. Thank you, aunt Emma, for being so wonderful!

Feeling tired. Will try to go to bed early tonight.

Good night my dear friends. Jana

4/1/14 day 85 after 1st chemo / Day 19 after 4th chemo

Had a hard time falling asleep last night, just thinking about life in general but felt better much better in the afternoon.

Aunt Emma and Uncle Charlie are being so wonderful to us. They took us out to eat and have drinks at Sally's in Somerset. We had so much fun! Thank you!

We are going home tomorrow morning. Starting to miss my dog Ruby! :) Jana

4/2/14 day 86 after 1st chemo / Day 20 after 4th chemo

Came back home from Monticello, KY today. We had a great time there! Thanks again Aunt Emma and Uncle Charlie for having us!

Got home and had yummy cookies and strawberries covered in chocolate sent by my dear friend Patricia Pugatch. Thank you so much Paty, you are amazing and I miss you so very much! I wish we lived closer to each other!! Love you!

Going to unpack and do some laundry. I am getting anxious for this next phase of treatments that starts tomorrow. Let's see if doctor was right when he said that it will be much easier!

I will let you know tomorrow! :) Jana

goodies I got from my friend Paty!

Sandy R. wrote on Apr 2, 2014 6:55pm: "Welcome home, happy belated birthday, and woohoo for the next phase being easier! <3 ya!

4/3/14 day 87 after 1st chemo / Beginning of Phase II of treatment – Taxol

Today I started phase II of my chemo treatment. I will be taking a drug named Taxol. I will be taking this drug once a week for 12 weeks.

Before they gave me Taxol, they also gave me: Benedryl 25mg, Pepcid 20mg, and Dexamethasone 12mg. These are medications help to prevent allergic reaction from Taxol.

The whole treatment took about 2h30min. During the treatment, I felt drowsy and was not able to do much. I dozed off for a little bit. Good thing that Joe drove me there and went to pick me up.

I got home around 2:30pm and was still pretty groggy. I ate lunch and went to bed. Slept until about 5pm.

It's 9pm now and I am feeling much better. If this is all I am going to have to deal with every week, I will be okay.

Thank you for all your prayers and positive thoughts. :)Jana

Julie wrote on Apr 3, 2014 11:18pm: "Thank you for letting us follow your journey, Jana dear. You are in my prayers."

4/4/14 day 88 after 1st chemo / Day 1 after 1st Taxol treatment

I could not fall asleep last night. I think the last time I looked at the alarm clock, the time was 3:59 am. On the other hand, I did not get up until 11 am this morning.

Had a nice birthday lunch with my dear friend Betty and my son Max, then spent some time at her house.

I am feeling a little tired and my mouth is dry but nothing compared to the side effect that the other drugs did to me. If this is what this treatment is going to be like, it won't be too difficult to handle. :) Jana

4/6/14 day 90 after 1st chemo / Day 3 after 1st Taxol treatment

I can't believe I am behind on my journal!

Well, we had a busy weekend. Let me remember what I did and how I felt: Sat - 4/6: Woke up super early (around 7:30am) and we headed to Indianapolis.

Had a great day at the Caribbean Cove Indoor Water Park. I felt great but really tired at the end of the day. It was nice to see Max enjoying the water and playing with other kids. He does not get to do a lot of things with other kids when he is off school, so, he had a blast! Jana

4/5/14 day 89 after 1st chemo / Day 2 after 1st Taxol treatment

Well, I wrote 4/6 before 4/5. LOL. Anyways, 4/5 was a Saturday. I slept until 11:50am! Much needed the extra sleep!

Felt ok most of the day. Went out for dinner with Kelsey, Max and some awesome friends: Josh, Melanie C. and Bill. Had a great time! :) Jana

4/7/14 day 91 after 1ˢᵗ chemo / Day 4 after 1ˢᵗ Taxol treatment

Visited the Children's Museum in Indianapolis with Max and Joe today.

I don't want to be negative but I confess that I was expecting more. Oh well, I do have high standards but for a $19.50 entrance fee and size of the place, I really expected to see more kids' toys and activities for them. For me, what they have there is pretty much the same what the Boonshoft museum here in Dayton has, but in a bigger scale. Now, if you are really into dinosaurs, then it may be another story. They do have a lot of stuff about dinosaurs. But I am not, so, it was okay. Max wasn't very impressed either.

I am super-duper tired. My legs hurt from waking so much but I feel great. I was missing this "tired for a reason" feeling. At least I know that I did something!

Hope everyone has a great week! :) Jana

4/8/14 day 92 after 1ˢᵗ chemo / Day 5 after 1ˢᵗ Taxol treatment

I would like to register some of the changes in my life after 3 months since I started my chemo:

Physically: I've gained about 12 pounds, lost all my hair, my eye brows and eye lashes are very thin, had ups and down right after the first 4 treatments, nose has been bleeding for the last week or so, although it may be the spring allergies telling me that this will be a rough season for my nose and eyes. I can't say about the long term damages that the drugs are causing to my body, I guess I will find that out in the future.

Emotionally: I don't know, it's hard to say. So many positives things have come out of this situation that I can't really complaint about anything. It may be weird to say this but I actually have been in one of my best moods in years!

I was at a stage of my life that I was praying for changes. God heard me. I believe that God has a plan for everything and this major change in my life made some of my dreams come true like for example that my mom would come to visit me. If it wasn't for this medical condition, she wouldn't have tried the visa again.

I was also in need of some time off work. I was tired and wanted to spend more time with my son and husband. This time that I've been home has allowed me to spend more time with Max and be closer to my husband. I also did things that I wanted to do and did not have energy to do before, like for example, to clean up my basement and organize cabinets and closets. I even learned how to crochet!!

Financially: Got some bills to catch up but I am very thankful for still having a job that paid for my benefits while I was on Long Term Disability. I know I will be okay.

Personality/behavior: Some believe that people don't change. The core personality may not change but I believe that people do change and I think that one of the changes that I am noticing is that I've been a lot more laid back with a lot of things.

One of them is with the household and laundry. They will always be there, so no rush anymore to get them done.

Spiritually: God has always been in my life. Nothing has changed in this area. I still believe that everything happens for a reason and that one day we will find out the reasons.

This is my last week of Medical Leave. I go back to work on April 14th. I am excited and at the same time apprehensive, but I am ready for a new challenge.

I know I won't have the time I have now but I hope that I will have more energy to continue spending time with Max and doing the things I like to do on my spare time.

It's time to go to bed. Got get up early to get Max ready for school. :)
Jana

Julie wrote on Apr 9, 2014 5:07am: "May God always bless you. Thanks for sharing your perspective and wisdom. Hugs to you all. ❤"

4/9/14 day 93 after 1st chemo / Day 6 after 1st Taxol treatment

Ops, I forgot to do my journal yesterday (4/9). I had a good day yesterday. Felt tired in the morning though. Had to go back to bed after Max left. But the afternoon and evening were great.

Bought the rest of the things that I needed to bake a big cake for this weekend and cleaned my kitchen so I have more space to work. I can't wait to see this cake ready!! :) Jana

4/10/14 day 94 after 1st chemo / Day 7 after 1st Taxol treatment

Today is a very special day! It's my mom's birthday! Happy Birthday Mom, I miss and love you very much!!

I felt tired again this morning but no "going back to bed after Max leaves" for me today. Instead, I went to store to get a few more things that I needed (and had to go back in the afternoon!) and started to work on some of the things I needed to do for the big cake! I also baked a cake for us, to celebrate my step daughter's birthday that was in March and we didn't have a chance to bake her cake around her birthday.

I've also decided to go back in the cake business. I just think that it's something I enjoy doing and the extra income can definitely help! So, if you need a cake, let me know!

My first treatment of this series of Taxol was on a Thursday but I changed to every Friday. So, tomorrow will be my second day. I hope that I feel okay again and that all I get is the sleepiness from the anti-allergy meds.

I will let you know tomorrow! :) Jana

4/11/14 day 95 after 1st chemo / Day of my 2nd Taxol treatment

Had my second Taxol treatment today. I actually felt better than the first one.

Got home and tried to take a nap but could not sleep, so I got up and started to work on the cake that I have to finish for tomorrow. I worked on the cake until 3am but then could not sleep until about 5am. Not sure if it was all the icing and left over cake that I ate that kept me awake or if there is something in the Taxol that does not let me sleep.

We will see how next Friday goes! :) Jana

4/12/14 day 96 after 1ˢᵗ chemo / Day 1 after 2ⁿᵈ Taxol treatment

Got up early, finished the cake and went to deliver it. Luckily, I was also invited to the party! Brazilian/American style. Good friends, cold beer, nice weather and great food! Had an awesome time! Thank you Star and Percio for being awesome hosts!

Cake I made for Vivi's 1ˢᵗ birthday!

Emmie Call wrote on Apr 15, 2014 5:55am: "That cake is amazing! It's very cool to look back at some of your first cakes and see how far you have come. So cute!"

4/14/14 day 98 after 1ˢᵗ chemo / Day 3 after 2ⁿᵈ Taxol treatment

Went back to work today. I work at CareSource Management Group. We manage Medicaid and Medicare members. I am a Team Leader in the call center. It is a very fast pace environment but the spirit is always good. Mainly, we provide support to members and providers but we are also always helping each other. There's a lot of team work and camaraderie among the staff so we can ultimately provide great customer services and enjoy what we do!

I loved seeing everyone again. The support I have been receiving from them has been making a lot of difference on my treatment.

My manager Laura gave me cake when I got there this morning. Yummy chocolate cake!

I make cakes all the time but I rarely get cakes from people and making my own cake is not the same, so, I really enjoyed receiving a cake from her today! Thanks Laura!

Got home and was very tired. It was a long day!

I guess I am going to bed early tonight, which is good because last night I could not fall asleep.

Overall, I am feeling great, just really tired, but I will get used to it again! :) Jana

Silvia Llacera wrote on Apr 15, 2014 7:36am: "Welcome back my friend. It was nice seeing you, even if just for a second. Love ya!"

4/15/14 day 99 after 1st chemo / Day 4 after 2nd Taxol treatment

2nd day back to work. I am so tired! My legs and feet hurt so much! I am not sure if it is the fact that I am at work all day or if this pain is some kind of side effect from this new drug (Taxol). I see my doctor on Thursday, I will ask him.

Other than that, my eyes are also getting really tired after a couple of hours of working on the computer. I guess I will just have to get used to the real world again! :) Jana

4/16/14 100th day after my 1st chemo / day 5 after 2nd Taxol treatment

Happy Birthday to my brother Hugo! Te amo meu irmao! (Love you brother!)

So, day 3 at work! I survived! At the same time that it does feel good to be back at work, interact with amazing people, help members, have a sense of accomplishment, on the other hand my life is gone again! I get home, I eat dinner and that's it. The day is over for me. I am so tired that I don't have energy to do anything else anymore.

The pain and tingling sensation in my legs have got to be a side effect from Taxol.

I did some research and I found out that Neuropathy is actually a symptom of Taxol.

I see my doctor tomorrow and I am going to ask him what I can take to help with this because it's just very annoying and painful.

4/17/14 day 101 after 1st chemo / Day 6 after 2nd Taxol treatment

I saw my oncologist today. I told him about my legs hurting and the Neuropathy. He confirmed that they are both symptoms of Taxol but he was surprised to hear that I am already having neuropathy. He said that it usually starts on week 10.

For the pain, he prescribed Dexamethason 1mg, twice a day, for the first 2 days after each treatment. It's a steroid. I will need to watch for more weight gain. He also said that I can take Ibuprofen or Aleve for the pain too. I bought Aleve today. I've taken too much Ibuprofen throughout my life already.

Things at works are going well. I am taking baby steps and trying not to overdo. I am getting less tired each day.

I am sad that tomorrow will be RN Stacy's last day. She is my awesome nurse. Well, she will be back but not until about 6 weeks. She is having a surgery. We will miss her. She is funny and caring. Thanks Stacy for being so kind with us! :) Jana

4/18/14 day 102 after 1st chemo / Day of 3rd Taxol treatment

Had my 3rd Taxol treatment this afternoon. Not sure how I am feeling. It was different from last week's treatment. Last week I got home and had energy to work, but not today. I had to lay down and after 3 hours, I am still a little groggy from the meds. I guess it can be because I've been really tired and had to wake up early to go to work this morning.

I am also having a little bit of pain in the neck LOL. It's a true pain in the neck. I am going to take an Advil to see if it helps.

The neuropathy (tingling sensation) in my feet is getting slightly worse. It does not hurt but it is very annoying. I hope I do not have it in my hands.

Today was the last day of my nurse before her surgery. She will be out for about 6 weeks. I hope everything goes well with her surgery. Pray for her. Her name is Stacy. Here is a cake I made for her. She loved it!

Hope everyone is having a great "Good Friday!"

4/19/14 day 103 after 1ˢᵗ chemo / Day 1 after 3ʳᵈ Taxol treatment

I woke up around 6:15am and could not sleep anymore, at least not until about 8:45am but then I had to wake up around 10:15 am to hunt for an "egg hunt" event for Max.

Ended up taking him to a church in Bellbrook with my friend Star and her family, which was very nice by the way, since my tentative to go to Delco Park to meet with friend Ana Paula failed because I was late and the "egg hunt" there lasted for about 2 minutes. According to Ana, the parents got more eggs than the kids, what a shame on those parents!

I was fine for most of the day but got really tired after a short walk at Cox Arboretum park. I got home and my feet really hurt. It's just a weird tiredness that I feel from my knees down.

I still have the tingling sensation on my toes which makes my feet feel even more tired.

I did take the steroids that the doctor prescribed, one pill in the morning and one in the afternoon, let's see if they will help. I am also taking Advil here and there to help with pain.

I am still making my hats and trying to coordinate them with my outfits. I finished one last night and another one tonight. I will try to post pictures soon!

Going to bed now. Good Night Dear Friends and HAPPY EASTER! Jana

4/20/14 day 104 after 1ˢᵗ chemo / Day 2 after 3ʳᵈ Taxol treatment

Happy Easter! Feliz Pascoa!

Had a great day! I went to St. Luke's Catholic Church in Beavercreek with Max and Joe. This is the church I used to go when I lived in Beavercreek with my host-family on my first year in America. There's something about that church that makes me feel very peaceful.

I've wanting to go back to church but I am not sure about the Concord church without the Rands. I feel bad saying that but it's true. I made really nice friends there but I really need to feel well inside a church that I choose to go. And lately neither Joe or myself were feeling like going to Concord anymore. I am sorry Pt. Tom if this is not the right thing to do.

Went to visit my host-father Gregg too while I was in Beavercreek and got to see most of the kids that I used to take care of, 14 years ago! Man, they are all grown-ups! Time does fly!

Got home and had a little bit of energy to clean the house a little bit but I did not want to overdo because I have a long week ahead of me.

I also talked to my mom today and she may be coming back in May to help me! Yeah!!!

Have an awesome week everyone! Jana :)

P.S. I keep forgetting to mention that my hair is starting to grow again, very little but I can feel it. :)

4/21/14 day 105 after 1ˢᵗ chemo / Day 3 after 3ʳᵈ Taxol treatment

So, my husband parked his car half on the grass and half on the driveway, behind my car, with enough space for me to back up and leave. Well, it's seems like my brain was not working this morning and I forgot that his car was there and backed up at full throttle and hit the left side of his front bump. I was very upset but glad that the accident happened even before I left my property. It woke me up and made me drive very careful on the highway.

But this is how I've feeling lately: I am operating at 60% of my capacity. Everything I do I need to be extra careful so I don't do stupid things.

Feeling tired all the time, physically and mentally.

I got home from work not too long ago, ate dinner and all I want to do is sit on the couch for the rest of the day. I need to go to the store to buy food but I have no energy. I wish I could do grocery online. Does anyone know a place where I can select my fruits, veggies, and other groceries product online and have them delivered to my house?? :) Jana

Silvia Llacera wrote on Apr 22, 2014 10:42am: "Hey, 60% capacity is good. Focus on the 60, not the 40! I backed up on Michael's car once in my driveway, that's fantastic that we can crash both family cars at once! Wanna give me a list, I can grab groceries for you. Love ya."

Sandy R. wrote on Apr 25, 2014 6:24pm: "I shopped for my boys online a couple of times when they all lived in Hollywood, but I don't know of any place around here. Like Silvia, I'm glad to shop for ya if you need me to. Just call or text me! :)"

4/22/14 day 106 after 1st chemo / Day 4 after 3rd Taxol treatment

Tired, tired, tired! OMG, I've never been so tired in my whole life for so many days in a row.

You know when you wear your high hills all day, if you are not used to it like me, at the end of the day you can barely feel your feet and all you want is a foot massage? Well, that's how I wake up feeling like, and just gets worse throughout the day.

Or moving day. That last day of moving. The day you know that you can't stop working until the old house is empty. Yes, at the end of the day you just want to eat pizza, have a cold drink and crash. Yes, that's how my days have been, every day, since I wake up until I go to bed.

I have no energy for anything and the neuropathy is getting slightly worse.

But I will make it!!!! One day at time and soon this will be over!!

Need to catch up on my journal. Later, Jana

4/23/14 day 107 after 1st chemo / Day 5 after 3rd Taxol treatment

Nothing has changed, I am still pretty tired all day long.

I've been taking Advil to help with the pain in my legs, it seems to help.

Good news is that I start working half days from home next week. This will help me a lot!

Hair is growing. I will start posting one picture a day to see the progress.

4/24/14 day 108 after 1ˢᵗ chemo / Day 6 after 3ʳᵈ Taxol treatment

Had a little bit of energy (after taking a nap) tonight. Went to Meijers and did some shopping for new shoes since everything I had was not comfortable for my poor little feet.

I have to say, Sketchers are expensive but they are the most comfortable shoes ever! No one beats them!

Max is going to the Columbus Zoo with his school tomorrow, I am anxious. :) I know, he should be the one anxious but he is only 6, well, 6 and 11 months, but the thought of him with a bunch of kids in a big place, scares me! :)

Will try to relax and sleep. been taking Benadryl to help me to sleep. Plus, it helps with allergies. :) Jana

4/25/14 day 108 after 1ˢᵗ chemo / Day of 4ᵗʰ Taxol treatment

Worked half day and headed to GSN (Good Sam North), well stopped at the house and Joe took me there.

My fave nurse is on a medical leave, she had to have a surgery and will be back in about 6 weeks.

At work, I preach to my team that changes are good, changes are inevitable, we need changes, etc... but I confess that I was a little nervous today because I knew that the nurse that has been with me since the beginning was not going to be there. I wondered how the new nurse was going to treat me.

Everything went fine. She was great too, I even learned some new things with her. I am going to continue preaching that changes are great, because they are!

Got home and tried to rest for a little bit. The steroid they give me during the treatment, won't let me sleep, I feel tired but can't fall asleep.

Now I am waiting for 5pm to go get Max at school and hear all about the awesome day at the ZOO!!

Happy Friday! Jana

Sandy R. wrote on Apr 25, 2014 6:33pm: "Love your honesty, Jana! Hope Max's day at the zoo was terrific! :-D Had a watermelon margarita and toasted you this evening. ;-)."

Jana Ratliff wrote on Apr 25, 2014 6:53pm: "Thanks Sandy for the toast, I wish I had a margarita today too! I also edited my post, you were probably laughing at my grammar errors and my sentences missing words... sometimes I just write and write and forget to read what I wrote before I click submit... oh well, I have excuses nowadays: I am on chemo!!! What's other people's excuse???? LOL

Jana Ramos-Ratliff

4/26/14 day 109 after 1ˢᵗ chemo / Day 1 after my 4ᵗʰ Taxol treatment

Had a great day! Despite the fact that I could not fall asleep until about 3:30 am and then was up at 7 am, I had a pretty good day. The steroid I get before my chemo keeps me wide awake on the day of my treatment.

Cleaned the kitchen, then went to the Vandalia Rec Center. Bought some passes to enjoy their indoor water park with Max. Their facility is great and the pools are awesome. I loved the whirl pool and little Jacuzzi they have right in the middle of the kids' pool. It was so relaxing.... I am not even having the neuropathy today. Once the passes are gone (10 visits), I may become a member for the whole summer!

Came back home around 4pm, had lunch and just chilled on my recliner for the rest of the day.

About to finish another beanie (red and black this time) and then bed time!

Hope everyone is having a great weekend!

:) Jana

4/27/14 day 110 after 1ˢᵗ chemo / Day 2 after my 4ᵗʰ Taxol treatment

Felt great during the day! Even went for a bicycle ride with Max, cleaned the house - a little bit - and cooked dinner!

But then I was really tired at the end of the day but still managed to go to the Drive In and watch Captain America and Need for Speed with Joe and Max.

Hair continues to grow. Here is the pic of the day:

4/28/14 day 111 after 1ˢᵗ chemo / Day 3 after my 4ᵗʰ Taxol treatment

I had a migraine at the end of the day. Not sure if it was the lack of sleep and just my regular migraine. Body aches too. I hope to have a good night of sleep and feel better tomorrow.

Sandy R. wrote on Apr 29, 2014 10:10pm: "Your eyes look fabulous! :) And look that cute li'l hair coming in! woot woot"

Julie wrote on Apr 29, 2014 5:12am: "I hope you slept better last night. Hugs my dear."

4/29/14 day 112 after 1ˢᵗ chemo / Day 4 after my 4ᵗʰ Taxol treatment

Thank you querida Julie, I did sleep better but still woke up very sore, everywhere. The bones and joints ached and my neck was stiff. Thank God for my lovely boss who lets me work from home on those days, otherwise I would not have made it to the office today.

In the evening, the whole family went to enjoy the pool at Vandalia Rec Center, I think aqua therapy is one of the best therapies for me. It really helps me to relax.

I will be ready to go to bed here soon. Boa noite! :) Jana

Julie wrote on Apr 30, 2014 5:53am: "Beijos, minha sempre querida!" (kisses my always dear friend!)

Sandy R. wrote on Apr 29, 2014 10:12pm: "So glad that aqua therapy helps you! Hope you have a great night's sleep and wake up refreshed. Boa noite! :)"

4/30/14 day 113 after 1ˢᵗ chemo / Day 5 after my 4ᵗʰ Taxol treatment

It's funny how we set our priorities to achieve our goals. For example, mine right now is to complete this treatment.

My task to achieve this goal is that I have to be in the hospital for my chemo every week, for 12 weeks. No questions asked. No matter what else is going on in my life, professional or personal, this is my priority and will be done, unless otherwise doctor changes direction or any other medical conditional trumps this treatment.

This is how we should set up our goals for everything in life. We should work to achieve our goal as if our lives depended on it. Do whatever it takes to achieve the result we need, no more excuses, no more procrastination. Work hard and be patient to make things happen. The saying "no pain, no gain" has never made so much sense to me in my entire life like it is right now.

And another month has gone by! I can't believe tomorrow will be May already!

Had to be at work all day today for a training. The neuropathy on my toes is pretty bad today. It's only 6:40pm but I think I am done for the day.

My nose has been bleeding a lot too. I think it's a combination of the Taxol and Spring allergies. I talked to the dr. about this last time I saw him and he said that it's normal.

Hope you are having a wonderful evening. And thank you for your support. It means a lot to me. :)Jana

5/1/14 day 114 after 1ˢᵗ chemo / Day 6 after my 4ᵗʰ Taxol treatment

Had a busy day at work with 8 new hires. Getting them all set up and talk about the job I did 6 years ago, is very rewarding. Their enthusiasm and energy of someone who is ready to embrace all the new challenges are contagious. I was supposed to come home at lunch time but I ended up staying there all day. I am tired but it was worth it!

Now just relax for the remainder of the day and be ready for another treatment tomorrow. After tomorrow, there will be 7 more to go! :) Jana

5/2/14 day 115 after 1ˢᵗ chemo / Day of my 5ᵗʰ Taxol treatment

"Everybody is a genius. But if you judge a fish by its ability to climb a tree, it will live its whole life believing that it is stupid. What is your genius? We are all capable of doing one thing better than any other person alive at this time in history. What is your one thing?" *Matthew Kelly - The Rhythm of Life*

I am still trying to figure it out what my one thing is. I love helping people to achieve their goal, but I think this is too generic. I believe that everybody likes to help someone when they can. I like to make cakes and I am seriously thinking about doing a volunteer work in baking cakes for underserved kids, maybe I will start with one cake a month. If you know any child that cannot afford a birthday cake, please let me know.

Had my 5ᵗʰ treatment this afternoon after a very busy morning at work. Another new hire started today and another will start on Monday.

Everything went ok with my treatment. My hemoglobin is up to normal level again. I've been eating more and healthier. I tried to cut down my food intake for the last 2 weeks but my hemoglobin went below normal levels. So, I decided that it's definitely not time to diet. Plus, every time I try to diet, I get sick. I really don't want to get sick. It's just that I can't be more physically active right now.

Took a nap after the treatment and then we went to Max's school for the "Englewood Hills Festival" - Max had fun, even won a Gold Fish.

Dinner at Steak and Shake, and now watching "The Hobbit", then bed time.

Hope I have some energy tomorrow to get out for a little bit. Boa noite, Jana

Julie wrote on May 3, 2014 7:11am: "Thank you, Jana. You helped me this morning. Hugs."

5/3/14 day 115 after 1ˢᵗ chemo / Day 1 after 5ᵗʰ Taxol treatment

Took my 2mg of Dexamethose in the morning after my 3 hours of sleep and felt great all day! Took another one in the afternoon and felt even better!

Went out for dinner with my friends Betty and Jim, then out again for some fun time with step-daughter Kelsey! Max spent the night at a friend's house.

Forgot to take a picture of my hair today. Had a too busy of a day!

Oh well, I will take two tomorrow!! :)

5/4/14 day 116 after 1ˢᵗ chemo / Day 2 after 5ᵗʰ Taxol treatment

"Successful people are in the habit of being disciplined. Undisciplined people are in the habit of being unsuccessful...Don't be a *do* person, be a *be* person. You are not a human *doing,* you are a human *being.*"

This is from "Rhythm of Life" from Mathew Kelly again. I just love this book and can't get enough of it.

He talks about why some people are successful in everything they do. It's not a mere coincidence, there is a lot of discipline and hard work in order to be successful.

Why sometimes it's easier to do make sure our kids follow a certain discipline but it's hard for us to follow our own?

Other times I feel like I am very good at following directions and I know that I am very responsible at work and deliver what I promise. Why can't I be the same when it comes to my personal life? Am I less important than others?

There is another chapter of Mathew Kelly's book that he asks a question: "If you had a million-dollar race horse, would feed it McDonalds or healthy food only?" Think about it!

I had a great day today. I guess the steroids are still in my body and it's helping to get through the day. I hope it continues to give me strength for the busy week ahead. I've heard that I will be hiring 20 more temps here in the next 2 weeks!! WOOHOO!!

Have a great week everyone! :)Jana

5/5/14 day 117 after 1ˢᵗ chemo / Day 3 after 5ᵗʰ Taxol treatment

Monday is always Monday!! Long day at work and decided to go out to eat the Dragon's Buffet since I skipped lunch. I was starving!

Until dinner time, I felt great! After dinner, we decided to go out for some spring shopping and I got tired. Everything hurt by the time I got home.

Now I understand why some people take steroids to do physical activity, it gives you a lot of energy and it's highly addictive. :) Jana

5/6/14 day 118 after 1ˢᵗ chemo / Day 4 after 5ᵗʰ Taxol treatment

My mind wants to write something inspiring but all I hear is my body telling me that everything hurts.

I woke up feeling tired and hurting already. How can one day I feel so great and the next feel like this?

I drove home at lunch time and worked from home in the afternoon. Bone ache, neuropathy on feet and the tiredness are just some of the symptoms of Taxol.

I want to take more steroids to keep going but I know it would be against doctor's prescription so, I will just take Naproxen for the pain and Benadryl to try sleep.

Things are going well at work. We got approved to hire more people. I am excited. I love working with New Hires. They are always so full of energy!

Well, I'd better get going... will be in bed soon tonight!

:) Jana

5/7/14 day 119 after 1ˢᵗ chemo / Day 5 after 5ᵗʰ of Taxol treatment

Had my 6 months check up with my breast surgeon, the surgeon who did my lumpectomy.

Everything looks great and I just have to do my mammogram in July and then see him again in 6 months.

Okay, the nose bleeding is really bothering me. I was ready to go to work after lunch and the bleeding started. Had to wait about 10-15 minutes until I was safe to drive again.

I got the office and called my nurse. She said that my platelets are good but she is going to order additional blood work on my treatment day just to make sure everything else is good.

I also asked her if I could see my ENT dr. to see what he says since I have a history of bleeding nose, she said that it's fine, I can do that.

I also asked her about my fatigue. My gosh, the fatigue with this drug is insane! I've never been so tired in my whole life. I asked her if I can take the Daxamethasone on Mondays and Tuesdays since those are the two days I really feel tired, she said it's fine too.

The hair continues to grow :) I think no more hats after tomorrow!!! :)
Jana

5/8/14 day 120 after 1ˢᵗ chemo / Day 6 after 5ᵗʰ Taxol treatment

I knew today was going to be a busy day and I was not going to come home at lunch time so I went ahead and popped 2mg of Dexamethasone in the morning.

120 days after 1ˢᵗ treatment and 25 years of celebration of my company: Happy Anniversary CareSource. Thank you for all you do to our members, community, and employees. I am very proud to be part of this big team. I truly feel like I get paid to do a volunteer work in helping people all day. The day goes by so fast and the sense of accomplishment is very rewarding! I am very glad I made the decision to go back to work even in the middle of this treatment. :)

Got to schedule me ENT appointment for next Wednesday.

Definitely no more hats after today! Look at how much hair I have!!

5/9/14 day 121 after 1ˢᵗ chemo / Day of 6ᵗʰ Taxol treatment

Here I go again, I am half way done with this treatment.

They were late today and I got to see a different nurse. I confess that I was a little annoyed today. The whole crew there today was very chatty with each other and loud. Oh well, I survived.

I got home around 4:30pm (I am usually home around 3:20pm) and tried to sleep for a little bit but was too tired to fall asleep so I got up and made dinner then went to the store to buy my cakes supplies. I have two cakes to make this weekend. I am still very tired but I hope I wake up feeling better to work on the cakes.

The hair continues to grow. Today was the last day I wear my hats. The weather is getting hot and I don't need them anymore.

Max has been taking piano lessons since beginning of February. I am so proud of him! Thank you, Ms. Lauri, you've been a great piano instructor and friend!

I am uploading a video of him practicing on YouTube. I will post the link soon. :) Jana

My son Max's playing the piano on my youtube channel
https://www.youtube.com/watch?v=3Pr7Wc27y3Y

5/10/14 day 122 after 1ˢᵗ chemo / Day 1 after 6ᵗʰ Taxol treatment

Again, I had only 3 and half hours of sleep last night.

Got up and started working on the cake I had to deliver tonight.

I wasn't in pain but I was really tired. Tried to take a nap around one but just managed to doze off for about 30 mins.

Finished the cake and rested for a little bit again before had to head out to deliver it.

It was a graduation cake. I am so proud of my friend Carman who has 7 kids and a full-time job as a Team Lead too and she managed to finish her Business Administration degree.

As some of you know, I went back to school a few years ago, and I know how hard it is to complete a degree when you have kids and work. Unfortunately, last year when I was diagnosed I decided to take a break but one my dreams is to finish my Business Degree too. I haven't given up yet, but not sure when I will have energy to go back.

Tomorrow is Mother's Day! I wish my mom was here but I know that she is in my heart as I am in hers.

And the hair continues to grow! WOOHOO!

Hope you have a great weekend!

5/11/14 day 123 after 1st chemo / Day 2 after 6th Taxol treatment

Happy Mother's Day to me, my mom and all the people out there who are a mother in one way or another.

The funny thing is that I never thought I wanted to be a mother then Max came along and changed my world. He is everything to me. He is the one who keeps me strong and fighting. If it wasn't for this amazing little person, I don't know if I would have the strength to keep going. Thank you my son for being you. Thank you God for putting Max in my life.

I had an awesome day! Finished another cake for a bridal shower, spent time with Max playing outside and had a wonderful dinner with hubby and son.

Felt good for the most part. I slept until about 9:30am and decided not to take the Dexamethasone today. I will save it for tomorrow. This will be a busy week. Hiring 21 more people to start on 5/19!!

Hair continues to grow!!

Hope you have a great week!!

5/12/14 day 124 after 1st chemo / Day 3 after 6th Taxol treatment

Monday dear Monday, you came sooner than I expected!

Had a great weekend but I think I really need to rest on weekends even though I feel great and with energy to do stuff because when Monday is here, I am exhausted!

The fatigue is just insane. No pain, but really tired. And I forgot to mention a couple of days ago, the taste buds are bad again. Not sure if it will get better or worse but I just can't taste anything.

On the other hand, the hair continues to grow, I am happy about that. No more hats needed in this wonderful and sunny weather!!

It's been really busy at work, if the fatigue does not get better, I am not sure if I can make it 6 more weeks.

I am in the middle of hiring 21 more people now, I may take a week off or so after this is done.

Well, I am watching DJango, according to my husband, it is a very good western movie!!

Have a great week everyone! :) Jana

5/13/14 day 125 after 1ˢᵗ chemo / Day 4 after 6ᵗʰ Taxol treatment

Felt less tired today, but I did take 2mg of steroids this morning.

I was able to get home and still do some housework - after I got a pedicure - ☺

Sometimes when I look in the mirror I do not recognize who I am anymore. Sometimes I even turn my head away from the mirror because I just don't want to see the face of this new woman. So many changes, internally and externally that I feel like I should even get new name and a new social security number, LOL!

I am just not the same person that I used to be. I am someone new and I am learning how understand and accept all the changes in my life. Don't get me wrong, I am enjoying this new person. She is definitely stronger and more confident. But still, someone new.

Deep inside she knows that this strength comes from God because now she understands that we may have our "wants" but when God decides that our "needs" is what really matters, there's nothing we can do to change that.

Today, I just live by Saint Francis Prayer and hope one day it will all makes sense.

Shanti, Jana

Lord, make me an instrument of Your peace. Where there is hatred, let me sow love; where there is injury, pardon; where there is doubt, faith; where there is despair, hope; where there is darkness, light; where there is sadness, joy.

O, Divine Master, grant that I may not so much seek to be consoled as to console; to be understood as to understand; to be loved as to love; For it is in giving that we receive; it is in pardoning that we are pardoned; it is in dying that we are born again to eternal life.

Sandy wrote on May 14, 2014 4:27pm: "I understand your feeling like a different person. I feel the same way. Tough for me to deal with at times, too. Can't always pin it down. Also, that prayer is epic! Thanks for posting it! Love you!"

Julie Schrodi wrote on May 14, 2014 5:25am: "Thanks for this, Jana. I was just thinking of this prayer yesterday, trying to remember the words, and here it is! You are in my heart and thoughts every day. Blessings to you on your journey. I cheer you on! Hugs."

5/14/14 day 126 after 1st chemo / Day 5 after 6th Taxol treatment

Tired, tired and tired but can't sleep. So many things going through my mind. I can't relax. I am always thinking about what's going to happen next. And when the weekend is here, I can't sleep because of the steroids.

Neuropathy on my toes are really bad today. I feel like they are cramping up on top of each other. It bothers me but it's not the end of the world. The fatigue is what really gets me.

Here is something I recently read from my favorite author Matthew Kelly that you may enjoy reading it too:

"There are four aspects to the human person: physical, emotional, intellectual, and spiritual.

Physically, when you exercise regularly, sleep regularly, eat the right sorts of foods, and balance your diet, how do you feel? You feel fantastic. You feel more fully alive. You're healthier, happier, and you have a richer, more abundant experience of life.

Emotionally, when you focus and give priority to your relationships, what happens? You switch the focus off yourself and onto others. As you do, your *ability to love* increases. . . and as your *ability to love* increases, your *ability to be loved* increases. You become more aware of yourself, develop a more balanced view of life, and experience a deeper sense of fulfillment. You're healthier. You're happier.

Intellectually, when you take ten or fifteen minutes a day to read a good book, what happens? Your vision of yourself expands; your vision of the world expands. You become more focused, more alert, and more vibrant. Clarity replaces confusion. You feel more fully alive, and you are happier.

Finally, spiritually, when you take a few moments each day to step into the classroom of silence and reconnect with yourself and with your God, what happens? The gentle voice within grows stronger, and you develop a deeper sense of peace, purpose, and direction. You're healthier, you're happier, and you have a richer experience of life.

Physically, emotionally, intellectually, and spiritually, we know the things that infuse our lives with passion and enthusiasm. We know the things that make us happy. *We just don't do them.*"

It doesn't make sense, does it? :) Jana

Sandy wrote on May 15, 2014 11:56am: "Isn't that what Paul the Apostle lamented about so eloquently - knowing what to do, but not doing it? Some things never change. :-/"

Julie wrote on May 15, 2014 5:19am: "Beautiful. Hugs"

5/15/14 day 127 after 1ˢᵗ chemo / Day 6 after 6ᵗʰ Taxol treatment

How do we know our limits? How do we know when to stop before we get hurt if we don't know for sure that we will get hurt?

Is it the doctor who is going to have to tell me that I need to stay in bed so I don't do anything else anymore?

One day I am fine, the next I feel like I was hit by a truck. Today was the latter. The body ache reminded me of my first treatment. I think this is the first time under Taxol that I experience such a thing.

I've been tired but not in pain. But today it hurt just to get out of bed to go pee.

Everything hurts: from head to toes... well, toes, I can't really feel my toes, so, from head to middle of my feet. LOL.

Again I am thankful for a flexible job that allows me to work from home, otherwise, I would not have made it to work today.

If it continues like this, I will be forced to take another leave but I do not want to. Things are going well at work, I am excited with the new team, hiring process, "fresh" and "eager to learn" people.

Everyone in this group is so unique. I really want to know them better.

I forgot to mention yesterday that I went to see Dr. Katz, (ENT), he just told me that my nose bleeding problem is just the dryness and that I need to continue doing what I've been doing: Vaseline, humidifier, and saline spray. So, I am doing it and it seems to be better.

Ready for bed, nite nite, Jana

Julie wrote on May 15, 2014 8:10pm: "Sleep well, my dear. May pleasant dreams refresh your mind and be followed by a Friday filled with energy. Love, love, love."

5/16/14 day 128 after 1st chemo / Day of 7th Taxol treatment

I worked in the morning and had my treatment in the afternoon.

It went quick today, I had the other nurse, the fast one LOL.

My numbers (hemoglobin, platelets, red and white blood cells) are all excellent!

Got home around 3:30pm, got to rest until about 7pm. Didn't really sleep but got to lay down and rest.

Max went to spend some time with his "American grandma" Betty. He is going to spend the night there too. It's his birthday on Sunday, we are having a small party tomorrow.

When I got up from my "resting time," My lovely step-daughter Kelsey took me to go shopping for Max's party. I am so glad she helped. I was still pretty tired and not sure if I was going to be able to drive.

Now I am watching a movie and will then hit the bed soon after the movie is over!! :) Jana

5/17/14 day 129 after 1st chemo / Day 1 after 7th Taxol treatment

Another 3-4 hours of sleep. That's how it's been going the first night after my treatment.

Got up around 7am, started working on Max's birthday cake and everything else for his 7th birthday party! Wow, I can't believe my son is turning 7 tomorrow! Max you are my Rock! You are the one who keeps me going. The one that has my unconditional love. Well, his birthday is tomorrow. I will save the Happy Birthday speech for tomorrow!

The party went well. Had 10 boys here at one point, then 4 left and 6 spent the night. They had a blast!

I felt tired and took breaks throughout the day but thanks to my friend Sandy who pampered with her awesome Mary Kay products, I was more relaxed at the end of the day.

My taste buds are totally gone. It's really weird but I still eat pretty much everything just see if I taste anything. I stopped putting more salt in my food though, I can't taste it anyways.

The hair is still growing, that's great!!

Hope you have a great weekend!! :)Jana

5/18/14 day 130 after 1st chemo / Day 2 after 7th Taxol treatment

Ok now I can say Happy Birthday to the most awesome child in whole universe! Maximus Yuri Ramos Ratliff, I love you more than anything else! You are amazing. You are smart, loving, caring, and I thank God every day for having you! Mamae te ama muito meu amor. Feliz Aniversario! (Mommy loves you very, very much my love. Happy Birthday!)

The boys got up around 9ish.. I confess that I could have used to sleep in today. I was still tired from yesterday but I had to get up and get going. Took more steroids, the amount that I can take after the treatment to help me to stay up.

Spent the day with Max, doing some cleaning and baking another cake for a friend of mine.

In the afternoon, we - including sisters Kelsey and Aliya - went out for ice cream and then to a park to let Max play.

Came back and finished the cake. I am done for the day. I have a long week ahead of me.

Hope you have an awesome week!! :) Jana

Max and his dad, Max and me and Max and his step-sisters Kelsey and Aliya

Julie Schrodi wrote on May 19, 2014 5:39am: "I hope you have an awesome week, Jana dear. Thanks for the pictures of the birthday boy, his crew and the cake. It looks like he had a terrific time. Hugs!

5/19/14 day 131 after 1ˢᵗ chemo / Day 3 after 7ᵗʰ Taxol treatment

Not sure if I will be able to walk tomorrow. I had an intense and long day at work.

My pedometer that usually hits 5K steps by the very last minute of the day, had 9K before noon today. By the end of the afternoon it had close to 15K steps. Boss was already warned that I am not sure if I will be in tomorrow. I may have to work from home.

Why did I walk that much? I had 19 seasonal employees starting today. Had to have them all logged in, settled down at their desks, show them around, resolve IT issues, etc... While this was a very rewarding day because I could see the happiness of having a job at an awesome company stamped on their faces, I know I overdid, I hurt all over, but it was all worth it!! They were very impressed with our facility and with their beautiful desks that they will not have to share with others - yes, some call centers are having their reps share desks with other people who are on PTO or called off - I am very excited to continue to work with them and see them succeeding!

I am loving my job! I need a bath now. Good night! :) Jana

5/20/14 day 132 after 1st chemo / Day 4 after 7th of Taxol treatment

Oh my word! Am I exhausted! This is a totally different level of being tired! The fatigue is insane! I could barely get out of the bed this morning. Thank God for a wonderful job that I have that allows me to work from home when I need to, because today was one of those days!

The neuropathy is really bad. I cannot feel almost my entire feet. I feel like I am dragging my legs when I walk. Five more weeks to go. Can I really do this with a full-time job?

Well, one day at a time. Ready to go to bed now.

Sweet dreams! Jana

5/21/14 day 133 after 1st chemo / Day 5 after 7th of Taxol treatment

Another long and painful day. The neuropathy is the worst now. It's a combination of pain with numbness. Not sure how I was able to remain at work until almost 4pm.

I don't want to give up and go on another leave because I know that some days I do feel great, but the days that I don't, are not easy.

I want to write more, I want to write about something that I am not sure what it is but I am extremely tired.

Going to watch Max play video game, then bed time. :) Jana

5/22/14 day 134 after 1st chemo / Day 6 after 7th of Taxol treatment

I could not wait anymore. My appointment to see my oncologist was set up for next week but I woke up in too much pain and numbness on my feet, so I called his office in the morning and they were able find me a spot for today.

He gave me a prescription for Vicodin for the pain and Gabapentin for the neuropathy.

I took them when I got home and went to bed. It helped a lot. I was able to go to work in the afternoon until almost 6pm.

I am tired again but I am sure I will be able to sleep better today.

Everything else was good. He is going to set up my appointment with the radiation dr. for the first week of June so we can get started on my radiation plan. :) Jana

5/23/14 day 135 after 1ˢᵗ chemo / Day of 8ᵗʰ Taxol treatment

Went to have my treatment in the morning today, 8am I was there. RN Linda saw me right away, my numbers are going up!!! My hemoglobin is at 13%!

Finished the treatment in about 2.5hours as the usual, then Joe came to pick me up.

Today we are going to TN to spend the weekend with my friends Aurora, Diego and their three kids: Mariana, Mila and Yan. They rented a cabin in the mountains (Pigeon Forge) and invited us to stay with them.

This is a place that I've wanting to take Max to - Joe and I have been there, but before Max was born, and we loved it, so this was a great opportunity. I know I should probably not be traveling and be focused on my treatment but I love to travel and I believe that a weekend doing what I like the most, is better for me now than staying home and doing nothing.

So, thank you Aurora and Diego for the opportunity!

We hit the road around 1:30pm, and after a long trip due to traffic, we got to Pigeon Forge at 8:30pm.

Everything was great, they received us with a Brazilian barbecue and much love.

As usual, on the days of my treatment, I cannot sleep, so we stayed up until about 4am. Then I crashed! :) Jana

Sandy wrote on May 25, 2014 3:41pm: "So glad you got a chance to get away, Jana! Perfect timing, I say! ☺"

Aurora Goggin wrote on May 26, 2014 11:11pm: "We loved having you Jana, it was so much fun :))))"

5/24/14 day 136 after 1st chemo / Day 1 after 8th Taxol treatement

Woke up early, around 7:30am and could not sleep anymore. Took the steroids to boost my energy and had a full day of fun with family and friends Aurora, Diego, Mariana, Mila, and Yan!

We visited Gatlinburg, had a nice lunch at Calhouns, then went for a ride on the Aerial Airtram to Ober Gatlinburg, where we spent the afternoon.

In the evening, we took the kids to ride the bump boats and then headed to Big Daddy's Pizzeria for dinner -yummy! -

At the cabin, had a nice Apple Caramel Martini - Thanks Aurora! - and then relaxed in the hot tub with the kiddos! What a perfect day!

Yes, I felt super tired and the neuropathy on my feet got really bad. I could barely feel my feet. Legs hurt too but honestly being with my family and amongst dearly friends, and seeing the kids' happy faces, was so worth it!

Thank you God for this wonderful day and please bless my friends Diego and Aurora for being exceptionally generous with us.

And the hair is getting bigger and bigger every day! I may have to shave it again in the middle of summer when it gets really hot outside! :)
Jana

Aurora Goggin wrote on May 26, 2014 11:14pm: "We had a great time!"

5/25/14 day 137 after 1st chemo / Day 2 after 8th Taxol treatment

Sunday, last day in TN. We had to leave the cabin by 10am, so, the morning was busy by packing and getting ready to leave.

Then we had nice breakfast at a local restaurant, said our "good-byes" and went our separate ways.

Aurora and Diego hit the road back to MI.

Joe, Max and I went to the Nascar Raceway tracks in Pigeon Forge and spent the whole day there. It was the first time Max got to drive a go-Kart.

At first, while waiting in line for our turn to drive, Max was a little bit scared and not sure if he could do it, but we encouraged him and he did a great job. Max has always been crazy about cars since he was a baby. When he was asked what he wanted to be when he grows up, one of his answers is a "race car driver". Now he loves to play Mario

Kart and Need for Speed video games and enjoys watching Nascar with Joe.

This place had about 6 or 7 different go-karts tracks for different ages and then some kids' carnival rides, such as mini roller coaster, spaceship, etc...and even a mini-golf! We spent all day there. It was fun.

We started heading back to OH around 5:30pm. We stopped for dinner at Applebee's after a couple of hours of driving and finally got home a few minutes after midnight.

Joe did all the driving by himself. I offered to drive for a little bit but he was doing fine. I was glad because I was really exhausted.

Got home, took a shower and bed time.

Again, thank you God for this wonderful weekend.

Pigeon Forge and Gatlinburg were places that I wanted to go for my birthday, a few months ago, but due to financial and health situation, ended up not going. And now just a few months later, You provided me with the opportunity to go and have a wonderful time. We just need to learn how to be patient and accept that everything in life has its season and the right time to happen. (Ecclesiastes 3:1).

And I also believe that "when you want something really bad, the whole universe conspires in helping you to achieve it." (Paulo Coelho).

And not forgetting about tomorrow's holiday: "Memorial Day." Time to remember the ones who died for our freedom. My sincere "thank you" to all American soldiers.

I know I wasn't born in this country but I do appreciate all the American people that I've met in these last 10 years who became my friends and family, and all the opportunities given to me without any discrimination that I really feel that by now, I am half-Brazilian, half-American. I do love Brazil and will always do and will never forget my Brazilian heritage, family and friends but I can't deny that America has changed my life and that even though I miss my Brazilian family and friends, I am happy here. :)

Have a great week everyone! Jana

Aurora Goggin wrote on May 26, 2014 11:17pm: "Mila was crying all the way back home because she missed Max so much. Hahaha I think somebody has a little crush :))"

5/26/14 day 138 after 1st chemo / Day 3 after 8th Taxol treatment

Thank God I do not have to work today! I am just tired and I knew I would be.

I know I have been doing things every weekend and then on Monday, I can barely walk, so next weekend I will not do a thing just to see if I will feel any different on Monday.

I just stayed home with Max all day, rested and played with him.

Did not even take my picture of the day. I felt really puffy and swollen. The doctor said that this was another side effect of Taxol but that it would go away after I am done.

Hope you have a great week, :) Jana

5/27/14 day 139 after 1st chemo / Day 4 after 8th Taxol treatment

I did not think I was going to make it to work this morning. It was hard to get out of bed and get going, but I did and I did have a full 9-hour day of work!

I worked the last 2 hours from home. Man, I was tired. After dinner, I took a Vicodin and took a nap. Got up, took a bath and was feeling a little bit better.

The new hires are out of training and starting to take calls.

I think that once they are all good to go on their own, I will have to walk less and will be able to work more from my desk or couch!

Sometimes I think about giving up and asking for another leave but I really don't want to. Please pray for me that I can make it through these last 4 weeks without having to give up and start all over.

I hope I feel less tired tomorrow. Nite, nite. Jana

Julie wrote on May 28, 2014 5:12am: I hope you slept well last night, Super Woman. ❤"

5/28/14 day 140 after 1st chemo / Day 5 after 8th Taxol treatment

Thank you, Julie, I did sleep well last night and I woke up a little bit less tired today.

Worked from the office in the morning and from home in the afternoon.

Even though I worked from home in the afternoon, I was super tired at the end of the day. But thank God this week is flying. I can't believe tomorrow is Thursday already, then Friday and I will 3 weeks away from the end of this phase!!

Tomorrow will be Max's last day of 1st grade! My baby is going to 2nd grade!

Julie, wasn't Tori in 1st grade when I met you?? OMG, he is growing too fast!!!

They will have a small celebration at his school in the morning that I plan on attending and then I will go to work.

Again, I am so blessed to have a flexible job and understanding boss that allows to attend all school events and be there for Max. Thank you Laura!!

Going to get Max ready for bed and going to bed too!

boa noite!! :) Jana

Julie wrote on May 29, 2014 5:13am: "Time flies, doesn't it? Max is going into 2ⁿᵈ grade and Tori is entering her 2ⁿᵈ year of high school. She flies to Brasil on Tuesday evening to spend a month with our friends in Vitoria. She is a young woman now having adventures without me. Thank you for sharing your journey with me. You are in my prayers. Beijos!"

Jana Ratliff wrote on May 29, 2014 6:10pm: "I can't believe Tori is going to Brazil during the World Cup! Lucky her!!! She is going to have the best vacation ever!!"

5/29/14 day 141 after 1ˢᵗ chemo / Day 6 after 8ᵗʰ Taxol treatment

Had a much better day today. I worked from home in the morning, went to see Max's "end of year" celebration - he made it to the Principal's list - Straight As all year long - then worked from the office in the afternoon. By the way, things are getting better at work in terms of walking less. My New Hires started to take calls at their desks and I can stay longer at my desk without having to run everywhere.

On the other hand, neuropathy on my toes is really bad... The medication dr. put me on that is supposed to help, Gabapentin, hasn't done much yet. He said that it would take about 2 weeks to start working.

Today is one week, since I started taking it. Let's see if I can start noticing any difference from now on.

I am home now watching Max play with Ruby - our amazing dog - and I may even have energy later to do some cleaning!

Hair is growing...it looks blonde on this picture but it's really grrrrrrrrrrrrrrray!!! At least it's growing! :)

One more treatment tomorrow and 3 more to go!! WooHoo!!

Well, I hope you have a wonderful Friday! :) Jana

5/30/14 day 142 after 1ˢᵗ chemo / Day of 9ᵗʰ Taxol treatment

So, this is how bad I want this to be over: I had a dream last night that I went to get my treatment today and they told me that they ran out of my drug and that I would have to skip this week and come back next Friday.

I just blew up on the doctors and nurses and said that I was not going to leave that place without my chemo, that I was not going extend my treatment for another week! It was a long dream with me yelling at everybody, LOL! Then I finally woke with a massive migraine that I had to take one of my migraine pills, Imitrex. Thank God I was working from home today. There was no way I was going to be able to drive this morning.

Worked until 12pm, then my step daughter took me to GSN and today was a different nurse: RN Stephanie. She was nice. She is an ovarian cancer survivor. She was diagnosed at the age of 29. She is doing well now. It's amazing how many nurses in that treatment center have had cancer. The nice thing about it is that they can really understand what we are going through.

My numbers are good again, platelets, red and white blood cells and hemoglobin is up even more! I guess those carrots and broccoli that I have been eating are working! It's funny how I am developing a taste for raw carrots. I never really cared for them but now I eat them for snack at work and with dinner almost every day, and broccoli too, but I've always like broccoli, not raw broccoli though... of course I have my share of chocolate after that. :)

Got home around 4pm, took a nap - tried to - for about an hour and then got up to eat.

Now I am outside watching the boys - Joe and Max - working in the front yard. Even with his back bad again, Joe has been working a lot in the yard to make it look better. He has done an amazing job with the flower beds, I can't wait to see them growing! I will post pictures when we they bloom!

The house really needs a deep cleaning but I am not going to overdo this weekend. I called the Pink Ladies organization and they are supposed to send me a cleaning crew next week as part of what they offer to breast cancer patients. I guess I will just wait:) But it's weird because I never had anyone that I don't know, cleaning my house before. I think I will end up cleaning a little bit so the house doesn't look too bad, LOL.

I am very surprised with the number of people that are actually reading this. I was not expecting that many people to read it on a regular basis. Every day I have at least 5-10 people accessing the website. Not sure who they all are - I know some of them who post comments and a couple of others who tell me that they read it - but I am not sure who the other ones are. I really appreciate you following my journey with me. I feel goofy sometimes writing these things but I really don't care. I want Max to be able to read this when he grows up, if he wants to, and know a little bit more of what I went through.

It also helps me. I keeps me positive, gives me hope and helps me to remember where I am in my treatment...LOL,

My friends from Brazil get upset with me that I am not writing in Portuguese. When this is over I plan on translating everything to Portuguese and give them a copy, and to my mom.

I feel a little bit depressed and nostalgic today but I think it's just my hormones - even though I don't have my periods anymore because of the IUD, I still get all the symptoms: migraine, feeling blue, no patience, and all that crap that we, women, have to deal with every month. Hear the tone? That's what I am talking about...LOL

I want to write about life but I have a feeling that's it's just not going to be good because of me being in a bad mood, so I will just try to be positive and smile! :)

Hope you have an awesome weekend!

And here are my new shades directly from Nascar Speeday in Pigeon Forge, TN!

Aurora Goggin wrote on May 31, 2014 12:30am: "Stay strong Jana, it's almost over :))))"

Tiffany Farmer wrote on May 31, 2014 1:33pm: "You are such an inspiration to me! I look up to you! I am here if you need me :)"

5/31/14 day 143 after 1ˢᵗ chemo / Day 1 after 9ᵗʰ Taxol treatment

Had about 4 hours of sleep. It's always like that when I have my treatment because of the steroids they give me.

Had a fun but not so busy day. Went to get my wall wine rack that was made by a friend of mine especially for me - will post picture once I have it on the wall - then went to have lunch with my American mom and dear friend Betty - Mexican food - yummy!

Came back home and rested for about 3 hours then went to finally watch "Frozen" with Max and stepdaughter Kelsey. It was cute but from all we hear about it, I was expecting more. I guess I do hold high standards. :(

Got home and decided to clean the kitchen. That got me tired, but needed to be done.

Now in bed with my little man - Max asked to sleep with mommy today, and how can I say no?? Joe is still at work anyways! :)

Have a great Sunday everyone!! Jana

6/1/14 day 144 after 1st chemo / Day 2 after 9th Taxol

Welcome June! What a beautiful day, 80 some degrees outside, felt more like 95 at one point. I wish I had taken the day off to go to the pool instead of cleaning the house to try to find my Iphone :(and still did not find it! It's been missing since Max's birthday. I do not use it as my phone anymore but it has a bunch of information and pictures that are important to me. For some reason when I access my ICloud's account, I can't see all my pictures, even though I pay for extra storage... Ahhh technology, it's being harder and harder to keep up with all the accounts, passwords, and this and that.... specially with the chemo brain!! LOL.

Anyways, I slept much better last night, from about 2am to 10am, I hadn't slept this much in a long time. But I still woke up more tired than when I went to bed. Unbelievable what this drug can do to our body. Intense fatigue!

Got up, had breakfast and took all my meds including some steroids that I am allowed to take up to 2 days after treatment.

Did laundry and some cleaning around the house, but not even half of what I wanted to get accomplished today. That's okay, I will get more stuff done tomorrow after work. Little by little I will get the house organized again.... and hopefully the Iphone will show up!

Joe worked in the front yard again, it looks really nice. See pics below. I can't wait to see the flowers blooming!!

Hair is growing, grayer and grayer, I am thinking about dying it, but not sure yet.

Hope everyone has marvelous week! :) Jana

Julie wrote on Jun 2, 2014 5:24am: "Your house looks so lovely and welcoming. I hope you find your phone. That is so annoying! Have a great week. Tori goes to Brasil for a month tomorrow at 5 pm. What an adventure for her! Hugs!"

6/2/14 day 145 after 1ˢᵗ chemo / Day 3 after 9ᵗʰ Taxol treatment

So, I was so tired yesterday that I did not even have energy to do my journal.

It was the same as every Monday. Worked in the morning from the office - It took all the energy I had to get up and drive there but I did - then worked from home in the afternoon.

I went to bed about 9pm - and pretty much stayed there until 6:30am next day.

Here is the pic of the day! Max called me "old grandma" because of my gray hair! :) Jana

Sandy wrote on Jun 4, 2014 7:25am: "LOL @ Max! Tell him I said to watch the gray hair comments. Haha"

6/3/14 day 146 after 1st chemo / Day 4 after 9th Taxol treatment

I can't feel my toes up to half of my feet, can't taste any food, body hurts but life is good. Just went for a motorcycle ride with Max in the back of the bike. I thought I wasn't going to be able to hold on to the bike, it's heavy, but I did okay.

I can't wait for this to be over and I just wonder if my body will go back to normal.

But this is nothing compared to what some people are going through. I just saw that a friend of mine lost her dad this week. I met her in the call center almost 7 years ago and recently became friends with her mom because she bakes cakes too and I had to order some cupcakes from her and while I was in her house, I had the pleasure of meeting her dad. We talked for a long time. He was so pleasant and friendly, just like the rest of the family. I can't imagine the pain they are going through right now. God please bless Rachel and her family. Help them through this difficult time of their lives.

Meanwhile life goes on and the old saying stays "Be kind to everyone you meet, you never know what kind of battle they are fighting."

It's bed time for me! :) Jana

Sandy wrote on Jun 4, 2014 7:26am: "You will feel normal again, my friend! Promise."

6/4/14 day 147 after 1st chemo / Day 5 after 9th Taxol treatment

Dear Lord when is this going to end?

I finally gave up on trying to be "super woman" and pretend that I am doing "okay" and decided to stay home resting today. I woke up 5:30 am with a migraine, body ache, bleeding nose, and could not feel my feet. I've been on Gabapentin for almost 2 weeks now and have really not seen any difference.

Most days, that's how I wake up and still go to work, and usually I feel a little bit better after I have breakfast and a couple of cups of coffee, the migraine is what really kills me. I think it is the rain. It's raining today.

Aurora, thanks for telling me about Joyce Meyer.

I finally went to her website today and here is what I found: Perfect for me! I tend to act upon my feelings and sometimes I wish I wasn't so impulsive and waited longer to make certain decisions. Hope you enjoy the reading below:

> "We all have emotions, but we must learn to manage them. Emotions can be positive or negative. They can make us feel wonderful or awful. They are a central part of being human, and that is fine. Unfortunately, most people do what they feel like doing, say what they feel like saying,

buy what they feel like buying, and eat what they feel like eating. And that is not fine, because feelings are not wisdom.

Feelings are fickle; they change frequently and without notification. Since feelings are unreliable, we must not direct our lives according to how we feel.

Negative emotions such as anger, unforgiveness, worry, anxiety, fear, resentment, and bitterness cause many physical illnesses by raising our stress levels.

***Trust in Him:** Trust God to lead you by wisdom, and don't merely follow your emotions. God will always lead you to a good place."*

Picture of the day: No makeup. What a difference, uh?

Emmie Call wrote on Jun 4, 2014 11:08am: "Beautiful no matter what! Rest up and feel better."

6/5/14 day 148 after 1st chemo / Day 6 after 9th Taxol treatment

I felt a little bit better today. No migraine, just the normal fatigue. I guess I am getting used to that too.

I ended up working in the office all day so I can work from home tomorrow morning.

So, I finally decided to clean up Max's toys in his bedroom, and guess what I found?? My Iphone!!!! Yeah!!! I found it!!

Now I can procrastinate a little longer on organizing my cakes' stuff because I actually thought the Iphone was lost in the cakes' tools and pans, but now that I found it, that can wait! :)

Well I am not done in his room... I'd better get back there and throw a few more things away before he sees it... the boy wants to keep every little piece of broken toy and every box or paper that comes with the toy!

By the way, the wine rack is ready for some wine! I am accepting donations now!! :) Jana

6/6/14 day 149 after 1st chemo / Day of 10th Taxol treatment

It's almost over! two more weeks and I will take a 3 week break then start on radiation: 33 treatments - or - 6 1/2 weeks, Monday through Friday.

I woke up super-duper tired. Glad I was already approved to work from home.

At 1pm Joe took me to GSN. My favorite nurse. RN Stacy, is back. She let me watch Netflix on her tablet.... she is nice and has a great sense of humor! She makes that place shine, everybody loves her.

I feel hungry all the time. I think it's the Decadron (Steroids). I've gained almost 30 pounds since I started this treatment. Not good. I am not happy about it but I guess I will have to just deal with that later.

I am going to try to rest now. Not in a good mood today, having a bad hair day, LOL.:(Jana

6/7/14 day 150 after 1ˢᵗ chemo / Day 1 after 10ᵗʰ Taxol treatment

This will be a day to remember for the rest of my life!

Max has an older brother, Joe's son, who has not been in our lives for over 8 years, which means that Max had never met him, until today. Although Max had never met him before, he knew about his existence and talked about him all the time. His dream was to one day meet Anthony.

So, today I went out for dinner with a co-worker, Stephanie E., my stepdaughter Kelsey, and Max.

We went to the restaurant where Anthony works. I had no idea if he was going to be there or not, so I didn't tell Max where we were going, I just told him that were going out for dinner.

For my surprise, Anthony was not only there but today he was serving (he is a cook but wait on tables some days), and he was the one who greeted us when we got there.

He was surprised too but very receptive.

We had a very pleasant dinner and a great time there. He sat with us as time allowed him to do so, he talked to Max a lot, and not even counting the wonderful company of Stephanie and Kelsey!! Thank you, God, for this wonderful day, miracles do exist!

Okay, my day now: I was actually able to sleep longer than what I usually do on the first night of my treatment. I was very tired last night. I slept from about 1:30am until about 7:30am. This is a lot for me on the days that I get my treatment.

Had a busy day by doing grocery and taking Max to Home Depot for the kids' project in the morning. Every 1ˢᵗ Saturday of each month, they have a little project for kids. I started taking him there last month. He loves it!

In the afternoon, I decided not to look like grandma anymore-nothing against grandmas but according to Max my gray hair makes me look like grandma - and had a makeover. Pictures of before and after below.

I felt tired but still well enough to do things but now it's 10:20pm and I think I am ready to hit the bed and be done for the day!

Hope you have a great Sunday! :) Jana

Sandy wrote on Jun 9, 2014 6:33pm: "So happy to hear that y'all got to spend some time w/Anthony! Max must have been thrilled! You look cute, btw. (And this grandma doesn't take offense. You're way too young to look like a granny!)"

Julie wrote on Jun 8, 2014 7:08am: "What a neat story! Thanks for sharing. Love the updated look. You are so lovely in every way."

6/8/14 day 151 after 1ˢᵗ chemo / day 2 after 10ᵗʰ Taxol treatment

Slept until about 8:30 am. This was pretty good compared to other weekends right after treatment but I was still very tired.

I had breakfast, took my meds and went back to bed for another hour then headed to Dublin, OH.

So, there's not much that I am scared of and trying new things is definitely not one of them!

A couple of years ago I found this hypnosis school in Cleveland and kept their information. Their website caught my attention because they said they could treat pain through hypnosis.

Recently I decided to check them out again and for my surprise they were having a class in Dublin and needed volunteers for their students to practice on. So, that's why I ended up in Dublin today.

There I met this very nice group of people consisted by the instructor and his wife, and 4 students.

My main reason for going there was because of my migraines.

They all asked me questions to get to know me but student Barbie was the one who actually worked more with me.

I was never totally unconscious, but she took me to a very relaxing stage and then she talked to my subconscious.

It was interesting and definitely relaxing. The trip was worth it! I am going back in 2 weeks!

Got home around 4ish and didn't do much for the rest of the day. I was very tired.

Hope you have a great week!

Anita Baldwin wrote on Jun 13, 2014 9:06am: "I went to a hypnotist when I was in Florida. When the session would be finished, I could feel the energy vibrate through my body for about 2 weeks. I went every three weeks for about 6 month and it was incredible. It wasn't the same as what you are going for but I hope it helps you as much as it helped me.

I hope you feel God's presence and love pouring down on you. I am sending many prayers your way. I am in awe of your strength and courage and that you can put a smile on your beautiful face every day. Have a good Day, Warrior Princess!!!"

Julie wrote on Jun 10, 2014 6:02am: "Cool! I will be interested in hearing how this goes!

6/9/14 day 152 after 1ˢᵗ chemo / day 3 after 10ᵗʰ Taxol treatment

Mondays, oh Mondays how I dread you during this phase of treatment.

It's just because my steroids are gone from my system and I wake up with no energy and pain all over my body.

I still went to work in the morning but drove back home at lunch time to meet with a staff from Molly Maids to give me an estimate on how much it will cost to clean my house. But here is the best part of it: Pink Ribbon organization is paying for 6 cleanings! They start tomorrow. I am so excited!

Then I worked from home in the afternoon and was done for the day. I literally spent the rest of the evening in bed. Took 2 Vicodins and I am still in pain and can't sleep.

Nose has been bleeding again.

Two more weeks and this will be over!

:) Janaina

Julie wrote on Jun 10, 2014 6:01am: "Oh sweetie, so sorry. Hoping this rainy Tuesday goes better. Hugs!"

6/10/14 day 153 after 1ˢᵗ chemo / day 4 after 10ᵗʰ Taxol treatment

I worked from home today. Body pain all day.

Neuropathy is pretty bad today too.

I am not sure if I can continue to work. Today I requested to reduce my hours until end of treatment, otherwise I will have to go on a leave again. I should hear an answer tomorrow.

Thank you for your support and your comments, I really appreciate it. Jana :)

Julie wrote on Jun 11, 2014 5:50am: "It will all be okay, my friend. You will see. One step each day. Soon you will be out of the woods and done with this chapter. Hugs and prayers for you.!"

6/11/14 day 154 after 1st chemo / day 5 after Taxol treatment

Had another difficult day. Body ache and headache that ran through shoulders.

Neuropathy is really bad that it's difficult to walk.

I worked from home again. I am so thankful for having such a wonderful boss.

I forgot to take a pic again. Will remember tomorrow.

Going to read a book (You Can Heal Your Life by Louise Hay) and then bed time. Good night!

Julie wrote on Jun 12, 2014 5:32am: "Dorme bem, minha amiga." (Sleep well my friend)

6/12/14 day 155 after 1st chemo / day 6 after 10th Taxol treatment

Took a PTO day today. I wasn't feeling well in the morning.

Went to see my oncologist at 10:30am. Everything is doing well, so well that he cancelled my last chemo. He said that at this point, I am not getting much out of each treatment and that not having the last one won't make any difference.

I was super happy because it will make a difference on my body in terms of the side effect.

Today was the opening of the World Cup, the most famous soccer championship in the world and it is happening in Brazil this time.

We went to watch the game at a friend's house. Brazil played against Croatia and won 3x1.

I had a difficult time falling asleep last night, I think it was about 3 am when I finally closed my eyes and didn't open them again until about 6 am. ;) Jana

Julie wrote on Jun 13, 2014 8:12pm: "Go Brasil! Go Jana!"

6/13/14 day 156 after 1ˢᵗ chemo /Day of 11ᵗʰ Taxol treatment

Today is the last day off my life that I have a chemo treatment!!! I have faith that I am cured and will not have to go through this ever again!

I want to thank all my friends and family for the support you've been giving me. You helped me to get through another phase of this treatment by sending me your positive message and words of encouragement, prayers, cookies, flowers, cards. I want to thank all the nurses who were wonderful to me, and all the love I needed!

I am here right now at Good Sam North and they just did my blood work and the numbers are great!

Ok, I will write more later. Jana

Aurora Goggin wrote on Jun 17, 2014 11:29pm: "GO Jana!! Com a Gloria de Deus essa turbulencia is OVER!!! Declare e profetize saude sobre a sua vida, out loud. "so is my word that goes out from my mouth: It will not return to me empty, but will accomplish what I desire and achieve the purpose for which I sent it." Isaiah 55:11

"He asked me, 'Son of man, can these bones live?'

I said, 'Sovereign Lord, you alone know.'

4 Then he said to me, 'Prophesy to these bones and say to them, "Dry bones, hear the word of the Lord." Ezequiel 37.

Much Love.

Julie wrote on Jun 13, 2014 8:11pm: "Wonderful news! What a beautiful day to be starting your life all over again. Love you. Hugs."

Anita Baldwin wrote on Jun 13, 2014 1:55pm: "That is wonderful!!!!"

6/14/14 day 157 after 1ˢᵗ chemo /Day 1 after 11ᵗʰ Taxol treatment

Slept for about 3 hours. Had to go work from 9 to 2.

Got home and tried to rest then went to a birthday party, my friend Keyla's party. We had so much fun! Keyla is very dear friend, also from Brazil and also a survivor of cancer. We've know each other for over 13 years and she is a great support in my life. I got home with a stomach ache. In order to stay awake at the party, I had a big can of redbull and some Pepsi. This was not a good combination.

Had stomach ache all night. Another 2 hours of sleep night.

6/15/14 day 158 after 1ˢᵗ chemo /Day 2 after 11ᵗʰ Taxol treatment

I think today was the worst day of my whole treatment. I woke up around 8am with vomiting, headache, and diarrhea.

It's Father's Day and I was supposed to go to Richmond, IN to have brunch with Joe's aunt and cousin but instead I stayed home, in bed, all day.

I am still not feeling well, not sure if I can work tomorrow.

Good night. Jana

Sandy R. wrote on Jun 16, 2014 5:26am: "I'm so sorry you're not feeling well. Do you think maybe it's the flu? Or is it chemo related? Either way, sure hope today's a much better day!!!"

Julie wrote on Jun 16, 2014 5:21am: "Good night, querida. Better day today. Gentle hug."

6/16/14 day 159 after 1ˢᵗ chemo / Day 3 after 11ᵗʰ Taxol treatment

Worked from home, felt a little bit better but was still pretty sick. Couldn't eat anything. I can't taste anything. Neuropathy is horrible. I am ready for this to be over!

6/17/14 day 160 after 1ˢᵗ chemo /Day 4 after 11ᵗʰ Taxol

160 days on chemo drugs. My body can't handle this anymore. I am so glad there's no more treatments.

I can't taste anything, I can't feel half of my feet. I gained about 30 pounds, I am exhausted all the time, bone ache...

But the good thing is that after all the side effects are gone from my system, I will be able to do anything I want because if even sick and hurting, I am still working, cleaning, and taking care of Max, and everything else, so I can't wait to see what I am capable of doing with my body working again!

I hope I feel better tomorrow. Today really sucked. The bone ache is killing me! Nite nite, Jana

Julie wrote on Jun 18, 2014 5:42am: "I send you gentle prayers and warm wishes for comfort of your poor, tired body. It has gone through a lot and has shown itself to be strong. Like you said, won't it be amazing to watch and feel it free itself of this toxic cure? Soon I predict you will feel amazingly strong and energized. I pray it is very soon. Hugs dear."

Sandy wrote on Jun 18, 2014 9:28am: "I echo Julie's sentiments. {{{Jana}}}"

6/18/2014 Day 161 after 1st chemo / Day 5 after 11th Taxol treatment

This has been one of the worst weeks of treatment. I say that because on top of not feeling well, I still have to work and even working from home, it's still work.

I don't even like to write when I am this much pain because I don't want to be negative.

Thank you Julie and Sandy for your positive comments.

Thank you all my friends and family who are praying for me.

:) Jana

Julie wrote on Jun 20, 2014 7:21pm: "Oh, sweetie. It's time to feel better for sure. It is your turn for fun! I hope it comes soon. Love, love, love."

6/19/2014 Day 162 after 1st chemo / Day 6 after 11th Taxol treatment

Today I went to see Dr. Rebecca Paessun, my radiation doctor.

I actually went to have a CT-Scan and mark the area that will receive the radiation.

I am still feeling pretty bad. Body pain, headache (which may be caused by the weather. It's been raining for the last couple of days), and really bad neuropathy.

I worked from home again after I came back from the hospital.

Nothing else is new. I am just ready to start feeling better.

:) Jana

6/20/2014 Day 163 after 1ˢᵗ chemo / Day 7 after 11ᵗʰ Taxol treatment

So, today would have been the day of my 12ᵗʰ Taxol treatment but as I mentioned last week, my oncologist cancelled it.

I am so glad I did not have another session. Although I am still feeling pretty tired and sore, I do hope I will start to feel better soon.

I had enough energy to go to the office this morning - I looked for you Sandy but you weren't at your desk - and saw my team.

While it was nice to be in the office and see everyone, I think I overdid.

I got home around 2pm and was really, really, really tired.

I will absolutely do nothing this weekend!!! :) Jana

Julie wrote on Jun 20, 2014 7:18pm: "Sounds like a good plan. Less is more! :-)"

Sandy wrote on Jun 20, 2014 5:02pm: "I thought I heard your voice! Sorry I missed you, and glad you're going to take it easy this week-end. ♥"

6/21/2014 Day 164 after my 1ˢᵗ chemo / Day 8 after 11ᵗʰ Taxol treatment

I can't believe I woke up at noon today! Sleep in is all I needed!

Felt okay until about 3:30pm and then I started to feel the bone ache again.

I still have the neuropathy on my feet. I am still taking Gabapentin that was supposed to help but I don't think I've noticed any improvement. I will keep taking it until I see my doctor again.

The taste buds are messed and I almost don't taste anything.

I spent the whole day inside the house, watching movies and resting but no matter how much I rest, the fatigue doesn't go away.

Hope to have a little bit of energy tomorrow to organize my cake supplies. :) Jana

Julie Schrodi wrote on Jun 22, 2014 7:36am: "♥□💗💞💓💗"

6/22/2014 Day 165 after my 1ˢᵗ chemo / Day 9 after 11ᵗʰ Taxol treatment

I had a pain in the neck - literally - all day today.

It's a pain that starts on the back of my head and goes down my neck and shoulders that is extremely annoying. I took Excedrin and ibuprofen but nothing helped... so by the end of the day I gave up and took another migraine pill - Imitrex - and I finally felt better.

I guess the whole hypnosis thing didn't work. Not sure if I will go back there this weekend.

Basically, my whole weekend was everything I planned on doing: nothing but resting. I think I watched 3 or 4 chick flicks on Netflix while Max re-discovered old but still new, toys in the basement.

It's amazing how he can play with his toys for hours without complaining. I remember when I was a child I was always telling my mom that I was bored because I didn't have anyone to play with...but then, I didn't have the number of toys he has, otherwise I think I would be happy too.

Tomorrow is Monday and I plan on working from the office!! I miss being there, seeing all the people. I like to work from home but sometimes I need to get out! :) Jana

6/23/2014 Day 166 after my 1st chemo / Day 10 after 11th Taxol treatment

As I planned, I went to the office today. I worked there until about 1:30pm then I came home. Had lunch, worked for another hour or so and then headed to a friend's house (Percio and Star) to watch the Brazilian soccer game. I don't think I have mentioned but the World Cup is going on right now and it is in Brazil. I am glad I did not plan on being there because I would have to cancel, but I do have several friends who are either there or traveling there soon.

Brazil played against Cameroon and we won 4x1.

I felt much better today. I think that aside from my monthly migraine that I yet have to figure out how to get rid of, I sense that I will start feeling better from now on.

I plan on going to the office again tomorrow. I hope I wake up feeling well!!

Going to watch a Brazilian movie now. Later, Jana

Julie wrote on Jun 24, 2014 5:38am: "Go Brazil! so exciting! Almost as exciting as you starting to feel better. May you feel better today...and tomorrow..."

6/24/2014 Day 167 after my 1ˢᵗ chemo / Day 11 after 11ᵗʰ Taxol treatment

Thank You my friend Julie!

I had about 3-4 hours of sleep last night. Not sure why I could not sleep but I woke up at 6:30am and was ready to go!!

I worked from the office today, all day! Oh my, I am tired! I think I will be requesting to work from home tomorrow.

Not much going on. Neuropathy seems to be getting a tiny little bit better. I am not sure how long it will take for the neuropathy to go away 100%. From what I was reading, it takes a while, for some people, it took about 3 or 4 months, for others, years.

The taste buds also seem to be getting better, I need to just pay attention now not eat even more!!

Going to watch Lone Ranger with Max and Joe now.

Good night, Jana

Julie wrote on Jun 26, 2014 7:17am: "It is a beautiful day today. I hope that it is a terrific one for you. Thank you for sharing this time with me and others. Your courage in the face of many difficulties is very inspiring. Love you."

6/25/2014 Day 168 after my 1ˢᵗ chemo / Day 12 after 11ᵗʰ Taxol treatment

What a day! I woke up sore, with headache, and tired, tired and tired! And that's how I felt all day.

The only reason I went to the office was because I had a new hire starting today and I needed to be there for her but due to paperwork, she didn't start today, she will start on Friday. I did come home at lunch time.

The radiation doctor called and they want to start on Monday. My first session is scheduled for 11:45am. Not sure if this will be time for all the other ones yet. I will need to figure it out how I am going to conciliate work and radiation.

I am ready to go to bed. I want to take tomorrow off but there's so much I want to do! But I will probably end up working from home if I wake up feeling like I felt today.

Soon this will be over. :) Jana

Sandy wrote on Jun 26, 2014 6:36am: "Soon, soon, c'mon soon! :)"

6/26/2014 Day 169 after my 1ˢᵗ chemo / Day 13 after 11ᵗʰ Taxol treatment

Exactly Sandy! Come on "Soon", where are you? I have been feeling worse than I was when I was under treatment. The pain in my body and the fatigue are killing me!

I worked from home today all day but tomorrow I have to go to the office in the morning, I do hope I wake up feeling better.

I've been reading about the side effects of Taxol and how long they will last and I am not happy. Some says that the fatigue can last for years. The neuropathy may not go away 100% ever. I think I will just have to learn how to deal with these symptoms from now on and stop whining but since this journal is supposed to document how I feel physically and mentally, I will keep writing about my pains until I see progress. :) Jana

6/27/2014 Day 170 after my 1ˢᵗ chemo / Day 14 after 11ᵗʰ Taxol treatment

I woke up a little bit better. Went to the office and worked until about 2pm. Came home and rested.

Went to pick up a friend at the airport in the evening and then went to another friend's house to help her with her iPad that quit working.

Came back home around 8pm, watched "The Voice", spent time with Max and then bed time.

In order to do all that, I took lots of pain pills: Naproxen, Ibuprofen and Tylenol are helping a little bit.

Vicodin seems not be helping much so I am trying to avoid it.

I am starting to feel emotionally drained because I can't do anything else. This will be a loooong summer for me. Patience, lots of patience, that's all I need to get through the next phase. :) Jana

Julie wrote on Jun 28, 2014 10:52am: "It sounds like a productive day. You are generous with your time and talents even when you don't have much energy and when you're in pain. It reminds me of the parable about the widow who gives when she has little. Jesus said that her two pennies were worth more than the treasures given by the rich. Surely you will be blessed many times over, my dear. You are an inspiration to me and I'm sure many others. Hugs

Mark 12:41-44"

6/28/2014 Day 171 after my 1ˢᵗ chemo / Day 15 after 11ᵗʰ Taxol treatment

I am a little behind on my journal but it's because I haven't felt any different in the last couple of days.

Saturday: I woke up tired and sore again. Rested for most of the day. Max had a birthday party at 6pm and he was going to spend the night there and with Joe working in the evening, it was only me.

I went for a long motorcycle ride. It felt good but then when I got home I was more tired. I just sat down on my recliner and watched movies on Netflix until about midnight, then headed to bed.

6/29/2014 Day 172 after my 1ˢᵗ chemo / Day 16 after 11ᵗʰ Taxol treatment

Sunday: Felt a little bit better in the morning. Went to the Vandalia Rec Center to enjoy the pool one more time before the radiation starts because I will not be allowed to get in a swimming pool during the treatment.

Got home from Rec Center and just relaxed on the couch for a couple of hours, then did some light cleaning and was tired again.

Went to bed around 11pm but had a hard time falling asleep. I think I am too anxious to start radiation.

6/30/2014 Day 173 after my 1ˢᵗ chemo / Day 1 of radiation

Monday: Today I started radiation. My first session was at 11:45am. It was weird. I was anxious and a little nervous. I cried during the treatment, not sure if the nurses saw my tears rolling down my eyes.

Just to think that I will have to this 32 more times was depressing. Is it really worth it? If God knows when it is time for us to go, why do we try to fight against that?

Oh well, I am only going through this for Max. He is my rock, my motivation to continue strong. I love you my son!

The whole process took about 40 minutes.

When I get to the hospital (Good Sam North), I have to scan a card that they gave me and head to the changing area. I then take off my clothes from top up and wear a gown and wait in the waiting area. It didn't take too long for them to come and get me.

In the radiation room, I have to lay down on this bed that is similar to a bed of a CT Scan.

I have to have to my arms behind my head.

They took some x-rays and then started the radiation. I did not see or fell anything.

I was laying there for about 15-20 minutes. The worst part is having my arms behind my head, it hurt to bring them down when it was over. I guess I need to start doing some stretch on my arms before the session begins.

I went to the office in the morning but will work from home this afternoon.

Tomorrow's session is at 11:45am again but then the other ones will be at 3:45pm.

Hope you are having a great day! and Thank you my friend Julie for your kind words! :) Jana

Matt Becker wrote on Jun 30, 2014 10:21pm: "Hang in there Jana! It is definitely worth it. You are an inspiration to so many people."

Sandy wrote on Jun 30, 2014 5:35pm: "Thanks for posting about your experience, Jana. Try to only think about one treatment at a time. Maybe that will help. God bless you!"

Julie Schrodi wrote on Jun 30, 2014 1:58pm: "Max is your rock. One step at a time, darling. It is all going to be okay. I just know it. Love you."

07/01/2014 Day 174 after 1ˢᵗ chemo / Day 2 of radiation

I worked in the office in the morning and drove to GSN at lunch time for my radiation.

Today's treatment was super quick since they did not have to take x-rays. I think it took about 5 minutes for the whole process.

I worked from home in the afternoon and then took my car to get fixed in the evening - the back bumper that broke when I hit Joe's car about a month ago and, I don't think I mentioned here, but a couple of weeks ago, my step daughter did the same thing I did to Joe's car, but instead of hitting his car, she hit my car. So, in addition to the back bumper, I now have the front bumper to get fixed too. Oh well, it's just a car. She was very upset but I didn't care. I told her that it was better that it happened in my driveway than anywhere else. She was taking her younger sister and Max to have ice cream when this happened.

It was another exhausting day. I see my oncologist on Thursday. I need to ask him if there is anything else I need to do or take to feel better. Not sure how long more I can handle working if this fatigue doesn't get better. :) Jana

07/02/2014 Day 175 after 1ˢᵗ chemo / Day 3 radiation

I worked in the office this morning.

Today I finally had the opportunity to sit down with some of my temps and do a quick one/one.

The first group may have a chance to get hired on as regular employees but when I told them that if this happens they will be managed by another Team Lead, 100% of them made this unhappy face and some of them even mentioned that they would prefer to stay as a temp then!

While that made me feel good, I did encourage them to apply for the permanent position and assured to them that they should not be worried about this.

I drove back home around 1pm, worked until 3:30pm then headed to GSN.

I changed the time of my radiation. It will be at 3:45pm from now on.

Today I saw my radiation doctor. Her name is Dr. Rebecca Paessun. I will be seeing her every Wednesday. I asked her to confirm the number of treatments and she actually gave a different number than what I had been told before. She said that I will be having 31 treatments - hey 2 less treatments than what I expected, I will take it!!!

Another super duper exhausting day. I want to take a day off but sleeping and resting don't help much, I wake up still feeling tired, so, I'd better work and save my PTO for when I feel better and can actually do something.

I am excited though for the 3-day weekend, especially because Brazil plays on Friday at 4pm. I confess that I was pretty sad yesterday when the US lost for Belgium. I had hopes that they would make through one more phase.

I am going to try to get some rest, it will be another busy day tomorrow. Boa noite, Jana

P.S. Thank you my friends for your kind comments and support.

Julie wrote on Jul 3, 2014 5:29am: "Boa noite, querida. Vitoria just landed in Atlanta from her Brazilian adventure. She will arrive in Dayton at 11:44 am. It will be great to have her home! Hugs dear one."

133

7/3/2014 Day 176 after my 1ˢᵗ chemo / Day 4 of radiation

I had an appointment with my oncologist today early in the morning. Everything is going well... well, according to him I am feeling exactly how I should be feeling. It is totally normal to feel this much fatigue and have the neuropathy for a long time even after the chemo is over!

Great, he just confirmed what I already knew by reading about the side effects of Taxol.

He also said that I will be on a chemo pill after radiation. I don't know why but I did not ask him for how long, I guess I don't even want to know.

I left his office and stopped by the Radiation office to see if they were able to go ahead and do my treatment since I was already there, and they did.

After that I drove to the office where I worked until 5pm.

Even though I was feeling super tired, I enjoyed being in the office a full day.

Resting now while watching "The Brady Bunch" with Max!!

:) Jana

Julie wrote on Jul 4, 2014 7:20am: "☺❤☐us♚"

7/4/2014 Day 177 after my 1ˢᵗ chemo / No radiation treatment - Holiday

Today is Friday, 4ᵗʰ of July, no radiation for me!! Or anyone else, LOL. It's nice to have a break.

So far, I am still not feeling any side effects. Maybe just a little bit of pain on my left breast. Both doctors (radiation and oncologist) asked me last week if I was having pain on my breast and I said no. I guess it's something that is expected because after they asked me this question, I started to pay attention and that's when I realized that I actually had a little bit of pain.

I've been using the lotion twice a day (they suggested Udderly Smooth Cream but I couldn't find it so I bought Lubriderm) and Crystal deodorant.

Crystal deodorant is made with natural ingredients. It doesn't have aluminum or other ingredients that are harmful to our skin. I wish I had found out about this deodorant long time ago. It can be used by anyone. It can be found at most drug stores, or WalMart. I found mine at Walgreens.

Updates on World Cup: Today Brazil played against Colombia and Brazil won 2x1,

I went to watch the game at the Dublin Pub with my step-daughter Kelsey and my Brazilian friend Manu with her husband Mark, it was fun.

After the game was over, Kelsey and I went for a long motorcycle ride. Melanie C., we rode by your house, but I don't think you were there. It was about 7:30 pm.

Overall, I had a great day. I've been managing the fatigue and the bone aches with Naproxen and only one Vicodin a day.

Looking forward to doing nothing this weekend!! Will try to just relax and maybe start some exercises. :) Jana

7/5/2014 Day 178 after my 1st chemo / No radiation treatment - Saturday

This journal is really helping me to keep track of things in my life.

Every day when I update the title by changing the date and number of days after my first chemo, it makes me think: "Gosh, I can't believe it's been that long already! Where my life would be now if this hadn't happened to me?"

I can't wait for this to be over so I can start a journal of my new life, a new me!!

But this journal is not only helping me to keep track of how I am physically feeling and sometimes emotionally too but it is also helping me to really think about the things I do in my life and how they affect me and other people who are directly and indirectly related to me.

Every day when I stop to write this journal I have to think about what I did and how I felt and in the process of doing that, other things come to my mind, that I don't necessarily have put in here, but that definitely help me to sort out the pieces of this big puzzle called life.

I did not sleep well last night, kept waking up and not feeling comfortable. I think I had a total of about 5 hours of sleep which is not enough for me.

Felt very sore and tired for most of the day. Took a nap in the afternoon and now I am listening to the World Cup game Netherlands x Costa Rica. The winner will face Argentina on the semi-finals. Argentina won against Belgium earlier today.

Exercises will not happen today but maybe tomorrow! :)

Hope you are having a great day! Jana

7/6/2014 Day 179 after my 1st chemo / No radiation treatment - Sunday

Oh Dear Weekend, why do you have to go so fast???

All I wanted to do today was to eat and sleep. Well, my wish came true. That's pretty much what I did until about 5:30pm. I was still so tired and my entire body ached but then somehow, towards the end of the afternoon, I got this energy from nowhere and decided to clean up Max's room and the basement. He helped me. I also did some laundry. I felt a little bit more productive.

I could barely walk after I was done but then I took a warm bath and felt back to normal, just tired.

I need to urgently lose weight! My oncologist said I can start dieting and exercising, so, I need to give it try. I am sure that part of this fatigue is just the fact that I have been very inactive and that I gained about 40 pounds. I know for sure that part of my depression, if not all of it, it's because of my weight gain, so, no more excuses, starting right now!

Have a good night and an awesome week!!

:) Jana

7/7/2014 Day 180 after my 1st chemo / Day 5 of radiation

I worked from home today, the fatigue was just too much for me to try to drive in the morning.

Did my radiation in the afternoon and came back home.

Did some light cleaning and laundry in the evening and then bed time. :) Jana

7/8/2014 Day 181 after my 1st chemo / Day 6 of radiation

Had my radiation in the morning, at 8:45am, then headed to the office.

Worked there until about 3:30pm then went to watch Brazil being massacred by Germany at a friend's house.

What a game! Germany just wouldn't stop scoring! Final 7x1 to Germany.

Tomorrow Argentina plays against Netherlands. The winner will play Germany for 1st and 2nd place on Sunday, the loser will play Brazil for 3rd and 4th place on Saturday.

Well, other than being frustrated with Brazil losing the game, I had a good day.

Was pretty exhausted at the end of the day, but I actually enjoy working in the office more than I thought I did. Working from home once in a while is nice, but I do miss the interaction with people. I am going to try to work more from the office from now on. :) Jana

7/9/2014 Day 182 after my 1st chemo / Day 7 of radiation

First, I would like to thank the angel who ordered the Udderly Smooth Cream for me. I got it today, I really appreciate you. Now, the doctor also told me that it would help me if I got that Ford Mustang Shelby GT 500 that the Ford dealership in Vandalia has for sale. It is the blue one. If you can arrange to have that delivered to me too, I will be very happy!! :) LOL.

I did not go to work today. I had very few hours of sleep last night and was too tired to get up and drive to work this morning, so I just took the day off.

And since I was home, I took Max to the swimming lesson in the morning and stayed at the pool with him until about 1pm. I was just watching him since I cannot get in the water.

Got home around 2pm, made lunch and laid down for a little bit before going to radiation.

It was different today. There's always two girls who position me in the bed and do the treatment. Well, one of them is on vacation this week, so there was another girl filling in for her, but today, the other girl needed to leave early, so, they put a guy to cover for her. I felt weird because my whole top was off and having this guy there when I am used to the girls made me uncomfortable. I don't know why, I shouldn't feel that way but I did, go figure!

I saw Dr. Paessun today, she is my radiation doctor. Every Wednesday I see her after the radiation. So far everything is going well with the radiation. No skin burns yet. The doctor advised me to continue to use the cream and lots of corn starch to protect the skin.

In the evening I had my dear friend Sandy R. coming to my house to pamper more with Mary Kay products. She did a facial this time. I really liked the products, especially the foundation. Thanks Sandy for coming all the way here to see me and to make me feel special!! :)

Ah, I keep forgetting to mention: My eye lashes are growing!!! Yes, I saw this tiny black spot on my eye lid the other day and I thought it was make up. I tried to clean up but it wouldn't go away. Yesterday I saw a lot more of those black spots, they are eye lashes that are growing!! I was very happy!

Getting ready to go to bed now and hope I sleep better tonight!

Good night friends, Jana

Julie wrote on Jul 10, 2014 5:41am: "I hope you slept deeply and peacefully. Hugs."

7/10/2014 Day 183 after my 1ˢᵗ chemo / Day 8 of radiation

Had a great day!

I woke up around 7am, went to work, had a productive day, and then went to radiation.

Took Max to piano lesson after dinner, got a goldfish for him that he had won from the school carnival, which he named it Silver, then went for a 15 min walk with Max and our dog Ruby.

It's been a long time since I was able to purposely go for a walk. It was great!

I feel like the neuropathy is getting better and the fatigue is improving too.

I did start a diet and plan to stick to it.

I still don't know who sent me the cream, but I really appreciate you. I've been using it and it's better than the Lubriderm. Thank you so much!

I am going to try to sleep now for the second time. :) Jana

Julie wrote on Jul 11, 2014 5:52am: "Awesome news! I hope your weekend is even better. Hugs!"

7/11/2014 Day 184 after my 1ˢᵗ chemo / Day 9 of radiation

Mornings are the hardest. I still wake up very tired and sore but when I get going and the muscles are fully awake, I feel better but then at the end of the day, I can barely walk again. This has been my physical routine for the past week.

I worked from the office today until 3pm, then headed to radiation.

Everything is still normal, no skin reaction, no pain - the very little pain that I had last week is being taken care of by the Naproxen that I take throughout the day - everything is going well with the radiation.

On the way home I heard on the radio that there was a Nascar fans' event at the Kroger's parking in lot in Vandalia. So, I got home and took Max there. We stayed there for a couple of hours. After we left, we stopped at Friendly's for dinner and then went to a friend's house in Troy. I got home around mid-night.

I had a great day but like I mentioned in the beginning of today's journal, I was super exhausted when I hit the bed, but it was worth it!! :) Jana

7/12/2014 Day 185 after my 1ˢᵗ chemo / Saturday-no radiation

Got to sleep in today, well until about 9:30am only because I wanted to take Max to the kids' project at Lowe's. I've been taking him to Home Depo on the first Saturday of each month but someone told me that Lowes has a similar program every other Saturday in the Summer, so I we went to check it out. It was super cool too. Max got to build "Turbo," the snail that races.

Then I went for a motorcycle ride. I forgot my purse at my friend's house in Troy last night, so I rode the motorcycle there to pick it up.

Got home and took a nap, I was extremely tired.

Later in the day, I took Max to a birthday party. My Brazilian friend Keyla's son turned 13 today.

I was exhausted, I think it was still from yesterday. I wanted to come home after a couple of hours of being there but Max was having a blast playing with a bunch of boys in the pool, then playing video games, etc... So, I ended up staying until about 10pm.

I was a little bit depressed today. It is amazing how being overweight depresses me. It depresses me more than the anything else I've been through. Why is it so difficult for me to either lose weight once for all or to accept that I will always be overweight and be happy and love my body the way it is? Good night, Jana

7/13/2014 Day 186 after my 1ˢᵗ chemo / Sunday-no radiation

Germany wins the World Cup, well deserved!!

Spent most of the day in bed. I am in pain today, more than on the other days. Don't know why, maybe it's because I did not take the

Vicodin last night, just thought I did not need it. To compensate, I ended up taking 2 today.

I am just going to take it easy for the rest of the day so I can work tomorrow.

Have a great week my friends, Jana

Julie wrote on Jul 14, 2014 6:00am: "Hello my friend. Courage, dear heart. Hugs."

7/14/2014 Day 187 after my 1st chemo / Monday - Day 10 of Radiation

The neuropathy is definitely improving but the fatigue and the bone pain not so much.

I felt pretty much like yesterday. Bone pain and fatigue. Luckily, I have a job that allows me to work from home otherwise, I would be jobless right now.

Things improved a little bit in the afternoon after my double dose of Vicodin.

At radiation, everything is still doing ok and I hope it continues like that! :)

Going to watch a movie with hubby now. Boa noite, Jana

Julie wrote on Jul 15, 2014 5:49am: "Boa noite, minha sempre querida. ♥" (Good night my eternal dear friend).

7/15/2014 Day 188 after my 1st chemo / Tuesday-No radiation

What? No radiation? Yep! I was on the way to the hospital for my session and they called me to cancel because the machine was broken. So, I went straight home, took 2 Vicodins and crashed. I was very sore today and have been like that lately. The OTC (over the counter) meds are not doing anything anymore.

Totally off the subject now. How many times have you done something nice and did not get any compliments or no one noticed?

How many times in your relationship have you thought that you are the only one who takes the trash out or prepares the coffee in the morning? Or feed the dog?

I saw a video last week at a friend's house and since then I can't stop thinking about it. In the video, she talks about doing things for her kids, her husband, and other people without getting a recognized every time, but at the end of the day she feels good because she knows she did the right thing and her life is better because of what she did and she focus on that instead of lamenting for not being recognized. This video has changed the way I look at things.

Have a good night my friends. :) Jana

7/16/2014 Day 189 after my 1st chemo / Wednesday-No radiation

Yep, no radiation again. I was supposed to go in the morning today because I had a meeting in the afternoon that I wanted to attend but they called me and said that the machine was still broken.

While I like not having to go there, I know this will just prolong the treatment. It's like snow day for kids in school.

I've seen a tiny bit of improvement on the fatigue but I am still very tired all the time.

The neuropathy is getting better too but the way I've been tired, it's hard to say how much it has improved.

Today we found out that one of our call center managers, the one who hired me 7 years ago for the CSR position and the one who hired me 3 years ago for the Team Lead position, is leaving us. She accepted position in another department. It will be sad not to have her there anymore, but I am happy for her. Becky, thank you for all you have done for me. For trusting and believing in my potentials. I will be always grateful for having you in my life. Wish you the best in your new position.

My temps continue to impress me. From the 28 temps that I had since May, I've lost 5 but 4 of them have already been replaced and will start on Friday.

I am still enjoying working with them. They are very hard workers and hold high standards.

I don't think I will be up for too long tonight. I've been having about 5-6 hours of sleep every night and this is not enough for me. I need a good 7-8hours minimum.

I am going to try to go to bed early and get caught up on my sleep. Good night, Jana

Julie wrote on Jul 17, 2014 5:58am: "Good night dear."

7/17/2014 Day 190 after my 1ˢᵗ chemo / Day 11 of radiation

I worked from home today. The fatigue was too much for me to go anywhere.

But tomorrow I have to go to the office, I have 4 temps starting.

I finally had radiation today. It was also the day to see the doctor.

My regular doctor wasn't there, she is on vacation this week. I saw another doctor, I don't remember his name. I think he was in the room for 30 seconds since everything is going according to the plan and I did not have any questions.

I also noticed that I lost 3 pounds when the nurse weighed me. WooHoo!! Baby steps but at least I did not gain anymore!!

I keep forgetting to register here but my nose hasn't bled again since the last chemo. I also stopped using the Vaseline since then. I do use once in a while the saline nasal spray when the weather is really dry. :) Jana

7/18/2014 Day 191 after my 1ˢᵗ chemo / Day 12 of radiation

I went to office in the morning as planned. All 4 of my temps showed up!!

They seem to be another great group! They are replacing 4 other temps that I lost mostly because they got permanent jobs elsewhere, but they were very sad that they had to leave.

It was a busy and very exhausting day but I guess I made it, otherwise I would not be writing this journal, LOL.

Got home from radiation and worked a little bit longer. Then it was "Mom and Son's Night." :) Jana

Julie wrote on Jul 20, 2014 6:03am: "One day closer to feeling great. :-)"

7/19/2014 Day 192 after my 1ˢᵗ chemo / Saturday-no radiation

Had an "ok" day in terms of pain. Took only one Vicodin and some OTCs.

I woke up around 8:45am and got the day going as usual.

Around 11am, Max and I headed to a Jeep dealership in Beavercreek to try to sell my jeep and get another one that is automatic. Mine is a stick shift and with the fatigue and pain, it would be easier for me to have an automatic car.

I test drove this beautiful 2014 red and black, 2 doors, 4x4 Jeep Wrangler that I fell in love with! I did not buy it. At least not yet.

I used to go "off road" with a friend of mine when I lived in Brazil and we had so much fun! I miss those times and I would love to have another jeep and find a jeep club in the area so I could learn where they go to have fun and take Max with me. He was super excited when I told him about driving in the mud, water, rocks, etc...

I am too impatient when it comes to buying things. I get emotional and don't think rationally about the consequences in a long term. So, I am going to pray about this jeep tonight and if it God's wish that I have it, I will have it!

Going to spend some time with Max and then hit the bed!

Good night, Jana

Julie wrote on Jul 20, 2014 6:08am: "We had a friend in Brasil who also loved Jeeps. I can see you and Max having adventures in a red and black Wrangler for sure! There is a Jeep Wrangler club based in Dayton. Here is their website http://www.muddybuddys.net/main.htm"

7/20/2014 Day 193 after my 1st chemo / Sunday-no radiation

Well, I haven't been writing on my journal not because I am in that much pain but because I don't have time anymore, I've been busy playing with my new toy: a brand new Jeep Wrangler Sports, Red Fire! Yep, I got it today! I thought I had died and gone to heaven when I was driving it home. I am not the only one who can't wait to go off road but a certain little boy is dreaming about it too. We are going to have so much fun!!

Bone pain level is the same. I've been managing with 2 or 3 Vicodins and Naproxen everyday, oh well, at least I am doing stuff, it could have been worse.

:) Jana

7/21/2014 Day 194 after my 1ˢᵗ chemo / Day 13 of radiation

I am so glad I am doing this journal, otherwise I would be lost on my radiation days LOL. Going there every day has become part of my routine. I joke with the girls, and try to have fun.

Today I took Max there with me. One of the girls asked his name and then she said: "that's so funny! I have a red jeep like yours and my son's name is Max!" What a coincidence! LOL

I worked in the office today all day, well, until about 2:30pm.

Things are about the same in terms of the pain. I wake up pretty sore and stiff, can barely walk but then once my body warms up and I have my first cup of coffee, I start to feel better. I do take Naproxen every morning, then again in the middle of day and at the end of the day I end up taking a Vicodin and to go bed either Ibuprofen or Vicodin again.

Got home from radiation and went for a Jeep ride with Joe and Max. We tried to go to St. Mary's lake but ended up getting a little lost in Shelby county that we decided to stop in Piqua and have dinner there: Buffalo Wings and Rings. It wasn't bad at all!

Got home super tired but it was worth it! It feels good to feel alive again :) Jana

Sandy wrote on Jul 23, 2014 12:30pm: "I love that you're feeling so alive! :-)"

7/22/2014 Day 195 after my 1st chemo / Day 14 of radiation

Wow, day 14 of 31 radiations! I am almost half way through!!

I worked in the office again until 3pm and then headed to radiation.

I had to let some of temps go, this is the one thing about my job that I do not like to do but needs to be done.

Got home from radiation, took Max to swimming lesson at Vandalia Rec Center, and went for another jeep ride with the family, this time we stayed around Dayton area. It was almost 90 degrees today, it felt great on the jeep!!!

Julie, I found the Muddy Buddy Jeep Club and submitted my application to them today to become a member, thank you!

Ready to go to be now. :) Jana

7/23/2014 Day 196 after my 1ˢᵗchemo / Day 15 of radiation

Wednesday, another long and painful day.

I worked in the office and went straight to radiation from there.

In the evening, I took Kelsey and Max for a ride in the jeep.

Got home and crashed. My body has been aching really bad. I've been taking Vicodin more than what I wanted to take.

One day at a time Jana, it will be over soon. :) Jana

7/24/2014 Day 197 after my 1ˢᵗ chemo / Day 16 of radiation

It took all the strength I had to get up and go to the office today. The fatigue seems to be getting worse.

The neuropathy is almost all gone but now I have this pain in my feet that makes me feel very tired.

Stayed home tonight and went to bed early. :) Jana

7/25/2014 Day 198 after my 1ˢᵗ chemo / Day 17 of radiation

I was too exhausted to drive to the office, so, I worked from home.

Radiation went okay. I am starting to burn, it's more like a red color, but it's not hurting and I hope it will not hurt.

Max went to spend the night at a friend's house, that gave me the opportunity to rest. I was in so much pain that I was in bed the whole evening. This fatigue has got to stop. I cannot continue to work if this doesn't get better. Even working from home hasn't been easy. :) Jana

7/26/2014 Day 199 after my 1st chemo / Saturday-no radiation

Woke up around 10:10am, then went to pick up Max at his friend's house.

Had lunch with my friend Betty and then stayed home for the rest of the day.

Joe did not go to work tonight, he was working on his car.

It was nice to have him home on a Saturday.

The fatigue continued. I had a few beers and it seemed to help. :) - but I can't drink every day, so, I will have to find another way to feel better. :) Jana

7/27/2014 Day 200 after my 1st chemo / Sunday-no radiation

200 days after my first chemo and so many changes.

Am I ever going to feel the same again?

I think it's PMS time. I've been depressed and thinking about things that I shouldn't be thinking about, like for example, what if something happens to me? Been crying a lot too. Stupid PMS! Why do we have to go through this every month?

I woke up feeling a little bit better but stayed very sleep for most of the day.

Finally, after 4pm I found some energy to clean the house. Vacuumed and mopped the whole house, now I am hurting again, but it needed to be done.

Going to soak myself in the bathtub with some Epsom salt to see if I feel better.

Good night and have a great week everyone. Jana :)

Julie wrote on Jul 27, 2014 8:11pm: "A bath and maybe a little chocolate are in order I think! No need to fear, dear sister. Cast your cares on our Father in Heaven. Let Him carry you tonight, dear one. Rest in his arms and sleep well. You are safe and loved."

7/28/2014 Day 201 after my 1ˢᵗ chemo / Day 18 of radiation

One more down, 13 more to go! I can't wait for this to be over!

It was another very painful day. The pain is mostly on my feet now. It hurts to step on the floor every time I get up. I called my oncologist and will be seeing him on Thursday. Joe said that it sounds like I have sprained arch symptoms. I don't know what it is but I had never felt this type of pain before. The closest I got to it was when I used to go out to dance in high heels. At the end of the night, or in the morning, my feet would hurt so much that I could barely walk! But in a day or so later, I was back to normal. What I am having now does not go away. No matter how much I rest, as soon as I get up, the pain starts all over again. Afff... it will be over soon, I have faith in God that this will be over soon!

Heading to bed. Good night, Jana

P.S. Eye brows are almost fully grown back up again!

151

7/29/2014 Day 202 after my 1ˢᵗ chemo / Day 19 of radiation

I worked from home today. The fatigue and pain in my feet were too much. I only left the house to go to my radiation and take Max to his swimming lesson and at the end of the day I was feeling much better.

Max has been fascinated about breasts lately. It could be because I had to talk to him a lot about them since I was diagnosed or it could be just a boy thing. He will not miss an opportunity to try to watch me changing, or "accidentally" touch them when we are cuddling in bed. So, tonight, I asked him to massage my feet because they hurt so bad and he did. He asked me to teach him how I wanted it done by doing it on his feet first, I did and then he did my feet. It felt great! I thanked him and told him that he was great masseur. Next thing I hear: "You are welcome mamae, and if you need a massage on your breasts too, just let me know!" :) LOL

Good night, Jana

Julie wrote on Jul 31, 2014 5:30am: "Boys! They just can't help themselves. ;-)"

7/30/2014 Day 203 after my 1ˢᵗ chemo / Day 20 of radiation

Worked from home again.

Went to see my PCP to get a refill on my Sumatriptan (migraine pill) and she referred me to a neurologist, Dr. Valley, to see if he can help me with the migraines.

When I was at her office, around 2pm, the radiation office called and wanted to cancel my appointment for today because the machine was broken again. I asked about the other one that I use sometimes and they said that they were all booked up on the other one. I told them that I didn't care and that I was going to go there anyways and sit there until they found a spot for me.

It literally takes about 5 minutes for them to give me my treatment I was not going to add another day to my treatment because they can't fix the darn machine. So, I did it. I went there and soon enough they squeezed me in and did my radiation. So simple!

After I came back, I worked some more and just stayed home.

I notice that I don't feel a lot of pain when I work from home but tomorrow I will have to go in. I have interviews to conduct.

Going to rest now. good night, Jana

Julie wrote on Jul 31, 2014 5:29am: "I'm glad you pushed forward toward your goal. Bravo!"

7/31/2014 Day 204 after my 1ˢᵗ chemo / Day 21 of radiation

I saw my oncologist this morning. I wasn't supposed to see him until the end of the radiation treatment however I ran out of Vicodin and he is the only one who could give another refill.

He said that the pain in my feet and rest of the body is because the nerves are healing and it is actually a good thing. Nothing much I can do, he gave me more Vicondin and I will see him again in 2 months.

I worked in the office today. Things are okay there. Lost a couple of temps, but already did interviews today to replace them. I really can't wait to feel better and spend more time in the office developing them.

In the evening, went to a couple of stores/pharmacy and stayed home for the rest of the night. :) Jana

8/1/2014 Day 205 after my 1ˢᵗ chemo / Day 22 of radiation

1 down, 9 more to go.

Worked from home today. It was hard for me to get up this morning. I felt tired and hurt all over, I almost didn't work at all, but I am glad I did. I actually accomplished a lot of things today.

I've been really sensitive lately, it's gotta be that time of the month! Ugh!!

Radiation is going okay, I can see the burn on my skin now, actually, it started to show about a week ago. The doctor said that I need to use lots of Udderly cream and corn starch from now on.

Not sure if I mentioned that my PCP referred me to a neurologist that does the Botox treatment for my migraine. The office called me today and scheduled an appointment for Sep/08. Hope it works!

Good night friends, hope you have a wonderful weekend!

Jana :)

Julie wrote on Aug 2, 2014 6:10am "Good night, my dear. Sweet dreams."

8/2/2014 Day 206 after my 1ˢᵗ chemo / Saturday - no radiation

So, this is a big day for me: I get to meet the Jeep Club members!!

I got up around 10ish, had my coffee, got ready and left to go to the site where the Jeep Jam event will be held at, in Wilmington, OH, about an hour away from home.

On the way there, I thought to myself: "are you out of your mind? At this stage in your life, with everything that is going on, you're are going, by yourself, to meet a bunch of people that you had never seen or talked before. You're nuts!" But I did it anyways. And I am so glad I did it. They were very receptive and encouraged me to try the trail and if I got stuck they would help me because I still don't have big mud tires.

So, I did the trail, and got stuck in one big hill, but they helped me. And by the way, I wasn't the only one who stuck in that hill, I heard later on that even someone else who had appropriate tires, didn't make up the hill without help!!

Got home sore and tired but happy!! Why do I have to like those things? Why couldn't I be normal? I remember when I used to ride my motorcycle more often, going on long trips, etc... I couldn't understand why I would go through rain, cold and super hot weather, and all the discomfort that a motorcycle has, just to get somewhere, spend the weekend, and then come back home. And do that again, again, and again, almost every weekend. Why? Why didn't I just stay home with my mom and brothers?

I remember one day, it was pouring raining when I was packing my bike to travel to another city for the weekend. My mom did not believe that I was going to leave under that kind of weather, but I did. I had to make several stops because the heavy rain, but I made it to the place in one piece! I just hope Max enjoys playing video game for the rest of his like, LOL.

I don't think my oncologist was very fond of me buying the jeep, he was too worried about me doing crazy things. I told him not worry about it and that if I am not on a restriction to work, I shouldn't be on any other restriction. Driving on I- 70 and I -75 everyday to go to work is much more dangerous than driving 5 mph in the woods. :)

Julie wrote on Aug 5, 2014 5:50am: "Never be normal! Play, play, play!!!"

8/3/2014 Day 207 after my 1st chemo / Sunday - no radiation

Yep, got the Jeep virus again. I say again, because I used do go off road with a friend of mine from Brazil many years ago, and now I got my own! Yes, besides the motorcycle, we did off road too. Her Jeep was a 1963 Willys, very slow and very old, and very uncomfortable, the top did not close all the way, which means that if it was raining, it was about the same as being in the motorcycle, but we had so much fun in that thing!!! OMG, we had a blast everywhere we went. If that Jeep talked... mmm... I am glad it doesn't!! LOL. Mary, I will never forget, (well, what I can actually remember LOL), our adventures in your Jeep or on my motorcycle. If there is a soulmate friend, you were mine for a long time. Our friendship was one to make many people jealous. Everyone knew that we cared for each other more than anything else. And I know we still do, even with the distance, I know we will always be there for each other. I miss and love you my friend.

Took Max and the neighbor's kid back to the Jeep Jam property, where I went yesterday, and did the obstacle course and some mild trail with them. They loved it!

Then took them to Cesar's Creek Beach and let them play in the water for a little bit.

Got home, and by the time I was done cleaning the Jeep and the kitchen, it was bed time.

I told Joe that now I have two houses to clean: my house and the jeep. :)

Julie wrote on Aug 5, 2014 5:48am: "Sounds like an awesome day! So glad you got to play. You are such a cool mom!"

8/4/2014 Day 208 after my 1ˢᵗ chemo / Day 23 of radiation

One more down, 8 more to go!

Had my radiation in the morning today because there was a meeting at work at 3pm that I wanted to attended but ended up being cancelled. Was not happy about that but kind of glad because around 2:30pm I was ready to go home. I was tired and needed to rest. I ended up staying there until about 3:30pm though.

Got home, took a nap then made dinner and tried to catch up on my journal.

I am starting to burn really bad. I told my boss today that I will be in the office tomorrow because I have 5 interviews but then will be working from home for the rest of the week and will definitely avoid the sun until treatment is over. I already had fun with the Jeep this past weekend, now I promise to slow down take it easy.

On the area where I am getting the radiation, the skin is very sensitive, red almost black, and sore. It's become uncomfortable to sleep and wear certain clothes, including bras.

Other than the Udderly Smooth Cream that my angel sent me, I use corn starch to help with the skin to skin contact. It does itch a lot too.

It's almost over. I will make it. :)

Thank you for your messages and positive thoughts. I can't wait for this to be over so I can start paying it forward what everybody is doing for me. :)

8/05/14 - Day 209 after my 1ˢᵗ chemo / Day 24 of radiation

1 more down, 7 more to go.

I went to work in the office today. Stayed there until about 5pm!! It was a full day of work for me.

The pain in my feet is a lot better, so is the neuropathy. However, I still get tired easily and have the bone ache and muscle pains.

The burning on my skin is getting worse and more painful. It is now hard for me to sleep on my left side.

Got home, made dinner and that was it for the night. I am going to work from home tomorrow. :)

8/06/2014 - Day 210 after my 1ˢᵗ chemo / Day 25 of radiation

1 more down, 6 more to go!

I worked from home today.

Around lunch time I got really sore. Went to lay down for a little bit and ended up having to stay in bed for a couple of hours.

Good news from the radiation people. They said that the last 6 treatments will not be in the area that is already in bad shape. It will be in a different area, more on the top of my breast. Thank God because I was starting to get scared of 6 more treatments in the same area.

I also saw my radiation doctor today and she said that my skin is actually not too bad for treatment #25 and to continue to use the cream and corn starch.

I asked how long it will take to heal, she said that it will be about the same amount of time that it took to burn, about 4-6 weeks.

Took Max to his piano lesson after radiation then worked for a little bit more on the computer. Took another nap, and worked some more.

This is the good part of my job. The flexibility I have to get my work done, is priceless!

Time to go to bed again. Good night, Jana

Julie wrote on Aug 7, 2014 5:54am: "One foot in front of the other.... hugs!"

8/07/2014 - Day 211 after my 1ˢᵗ chemo / Day 26 of radiation

1 more down, 5 more to go!

I worked from home today.

Still having bone pain. I've been taking naproxen, ibuprofen, and two vicodins a day.

The pain in my left breast had also increased.

It's uncomfortable to sleep now.

Not sure why but I felt blue today. I can't wait for this to be over.

Better days will come, I have faith that they will!

Good night, Jana

8/08/20714 - Day 212 after my 1ˢᵗ chemo / Day 27 of radiation

Friday - one more down, 4 more to go!

Worked from home again.

The body pain continues and the area affected by the radiation is getting more painful. It will soon be over!! Jana

8/09/2014 - Day 213 after my 1ˢᵗ chemo / Saturday - no radiation

Woke up super early today as I had my "All Staff" meeting at the Greene shopping center to go.

The meeting was done about 11:15am. Headed home. Later on, I went to have lunch with a co-worker, Stephanie E., at a Mexican restaurant.

Left the restaurant and was heading home. Joe called to inform me that he had wrecked his car and was being taken to the hospital.

I went to see him at Good Sam Hospital. He was fine but they still did a CT scan to make sure he was fine. He was released around 11pm.

It was a long day but thank God he was ok. I went to bed but had a hard time falling asleep.

Julie wrote on Aug 12, 2014 5:24am: "Wow! Glad Joe was ok! That is scary!"

8/10/2014 - Day 214 after my 1ˢᵗ chemo / Sunday - no radiation

We went to see Joe's car at the junk yard. It's probably going to be totaled. He is upset, he loved that car, but again, we are glad that he is ok.

I was in pain most of the day. I guess it was because I did not sleep well last night and had a migraine that I ended up having to take one of my migraine pills.

Towards the end of the day, Max, Kelsey and I went to the Englewood Festival for about an hour. We've been living in Englewood for 4 years and this is the first year that I go to the Festival. It was okay. I would have been better if it wasn't too hot, or if I wasn't on radiation.

Got home and just had a lazy evening. Went to bed around 11pm as I was still in pain.

8/11/2014 - Day 215 after my 1ˢᵗ chemo / Day 28 of radiation

28 down, 3 more to go! I am almost there!!!

I woke up not feeling well. I almost called off today but I am glad I did not. I ended up feeling better after my first cup of coffee but still had a light migraine which was treated with Tylenol migraine. I really try to avoid taking my migraine pill because it makes me sick of my stomach.

Had lunch with Lauri Schwalm (Max's piano instructor) and our Pastor Liz Rand. It was a nice treat to see you Pastor Liz. I really wish you didn't have to move but I am happy that you and your family are doing well. And thank you Lauri for lunch and for providing this wonderful opportunity for me and Max to see Pastor Liz again! :)

Had my radiation, came home and worked until almost 6pm.

Took a nap after dinner and now I hope I can fall asleep again. :)

I took only one Vicodin today. I hope not have to take another one. The constipation I am getting from it is not fun. Jana :)

Julie wrote on Aug 12, 2014 5:16am: "Hugs and hopes for a great day today!"

8/12/2014 - Day 216 after my 1ˢᵗ chemo / Day 29 of radiation

29 down, 2 more to go!!!

Again, morning was the hardest period of the day. Getting out of bed was not fun, but I did it.

Worked from home all day and still found some energy to do some cleaning in the evening.

I do like to work from home but I am ready to go back to the office. I can't wait to go back with full force and work with all my 28 temps!!!

2 more days and the treatment will be over. I can't wait for that!!

The burnt hasn't gotten any worse, it is okay, manageable with my angel's cream and corn starch.

I feel like watching a moving tonight, maybe I will put the boy in bed and try to watch something on Netflix, if don't fall asleep. :)

Julie wrote on Aug 13, 2014 5:23am: "Always love your smile. Hugs!"

8/13/14 - Day 217 after my 1ˢᵗ chemo / Day 30 of radiation

The pain is definitely improving. It's 9:15pm and all I had today was 600mg of Naproxen. Nothing else! Okay, I had 2 beers this evening. That may have helped with the pain too. But seriously, it's seems like it is getting better!!

Penultimo day of radiation! That's the word in Portuguese for before the last of anything.

I worked from home today again and at the expected time, drove to GSN. Took Max with me today. Had my treatment and saw Dr. Paessun today. She already discharged me and gave me the instructions on how to take care of the burn: just keep washing and when the pain is over, I can start scrubbing the dead skin to make room for the new skin.

Came back home, worked some more, and then went to have dinner with Joe while Max attended the Vacation Bible School at Concord Methodist church.

I am so excited for tomorrow that I don't even think I will sleep well tonight!!!

Thank you my friends for all your support!!
beijos! Jana

Emmie Call wrote on Aug 14, 2014 5:56am: "Congratulations Jana! I'm so happy that this part of your journey is over!"
Julie wrote on Aug 14, 2014 5:25am: "Praise be to God! Thanks for the smile to start my day! 😊 Hugs!"

8/14/14 - Day 218 after my 1st chemo / Day 31 and last day of radiation!!!

I did it!!
218 days of treatment to reduce the chances of the tumor to come back.

Thank you my friends, family, and others that don't know me but somehow helped me in this journey.

There is a feeling of emptiness right now. It seems like the mission was accomplished and now what? I guess I could start working on losing weight.

We will see!

I am not sure if I will be writing as often as I did anymore. Maybe here and there when I see a doctor or do a test.

Thank you again and may God bless you.

com amor, Jana (with love, Jana)

Julie wrote on Aug 15, 2014 5:50am: "Happy day, Jana. Many blessings as you walk out of this difficult path onto one which is hopefully smoother, sunnier and more fun. (Maybe I should say RIDE out with that pretty red Jeep!)"
Sandy wrote on Aug 15, 2014 5:07am: "Yea! Party time! Way to hang in there through all of this, Jana banana! And, thanks for sharing your journey here with us. Your honesty and candor are a light breeze on a sultry day. God bless you, and welcome to remission. :)"
Matt Becker wrote on Aug 14, 2014 9:25pm: "Congratulations Jana! You are such an inspiration and I am so happy for you!"

Jana Ratliff Aug 14, 2014 10:09pm

Thank you, Julie, Sandy, and Matt for your kind comments. I only knew how strong I was when being strong was all I had left. But I couldn't haven't done alone. Thank you again!

Jana Ramos-Ratliff

8/18/14 / Day 1 of the rest of my life. Phase IV: dieting and exercising

Keeping a journal during my chemo and radiation treatments helped me to get through the most difficult time of my life. It was like a therapy for me. I am not sure how it would have been without the journal and all the support I got from friends and family. The journal kept me positive and aware of my progress and that's why I decided to continue to write as I am determined to face what I would call the second most difficult challenge of my life: dieting and exercising. I like to eat and I don't like to exercise. I've never been a really small person. I am 5'5" (1,65m) and 150 pounds was what I weighed when I came back to the USA 10 years ago. Except when I was pregnant, this is the heaviest I've been since then: 210 pounds. During the cancer treatment I gained about 40 pounds. People don't understand how I gained weight mostly during the chemo treatment when most of people, lose. The answer is simple: not enough energy to do anything, especially during a severe winter when the weather was below zero for the most part and constantly eating the wrong food because all I could taste was extremely sweets (chocolate and ice cream) and always adding more salt to the other things that I tried to eat. I was afraid of not eating enough calories and being weak and increasing the chances of me getting sick, so, I just ate what I could taste a little bit. But the good news is that I am feeling better and better each day that I can start losing what I gained plus whatever I need to lose to go back to around 150 again. Today is day one: 95.7 kg. 210 pounds 50 min on tread mill. 2.526miles 300 calories.

I hope you enjoyed following my journey with me and that somehow, I also inspired you to be a better version of yourself. And one last thought: never lose hope. Even when everything is falling apart, try to find the reasons you still have to smile, also, helping other people usually makes you forget about your own problems, it is an awesome feeling!

Julie wrote on Aug 18, 2014 2:57pm: "I am on the same journey, my dear. Let's encourage each other. Day 1 for me! So far so good. :-)
Jana Ratliff wrote on Aug 18, 2014 6:52pm" We can do it Julie!"

Thank you for reading my journal and remember always: "Whether you think you can or you think you can't – you are right!" *(Henry Ford)*

Male Breast Cancer Awareness

I want to say a special thank you to a male friend for sharing his story with me. I also hope this brings awareness to all men out there. This friend shared with me that he not only had breast cancer once but twice. I will let him share his experience with male breast cancer. The hope is that we may let our male friends and partners know that breast cancer is a real possibility for men.

"One day while I was shaving I noticed fresh blood on my forearm. For a couple of weeks I had noticed small blood spots on the sheet of the bed but couldn't find any cuts or scrapes on my body. I washed the blood off and continued shaving, only to see more bright red blood on my forearm. It was then I noted blood was dripping from my right nipple.

I saw a doctor who related males have about a marble size amount of breast tissue just behind the nipples. The suggestion was to remove the tissue, which was done during a small surgical process. All seemed well after that. I was 34 years old at that time.

Fifteen years later, at age 49, I was showering and noticed my chest on the right side was more firm than the left. For the next two weeks, I continued to monitor the area and noted an enlargement and more firmness. I spoke with two different doctors that assured me it was nothing to worry about and asked if perhaps I had fallen or had an accident and this could be a contusion and tissue that had swollen. I was certain I had not injured myself. After three more weeks and noting the area was getting larger and firmer, I saw a different doctor who referred me to a female breast surgeon. She immediately suspected it was a cancerous mass. Within the same week she performed a lumpectomy and a week later, pathology indicated the mass was malignant. The doctor wasted no time explaining the only sure way to catch the cancer was to perform a modified radical mastectomy of the area, and to take 25 lymph nodes for analysis. Within a week she performed the operation. She explained the mastectomy was the best course of action as even leaving one cancerous cell behind would result in the eventual progression of the disease. She added that 15 years ago, when doctors had removed the male breast tissue, they did not get all the cancerous cells and that is why the cancer had surfaced. She added the cells can lay dormant for years and be triggered by any of several events.

Following surgery and recovery, I underwent treatment and was given tamoxifen for five years. After the five years, I was advised I no longer needed to take the medication. I was genetically tested to see if I carried a gene that would predispose my children to cancer and fortunately the result came back negative.

In consultation with my surgeon and oncologist, they related the occurrence of male breast cancer is extremely rare and males tend not to be as proactive in seeing a doctor about a condition that appears abnormal. They also related there is little information on the treatment of male breast cancer and doctors typically follow the same regimen as they do for women.

I will say that mental attitude played a large part in my approach toward dealing with the cancer and my recovery. When I was diagnosed, I advised my friends and family and of course my working associates. Clearly I would be out of the office for surgery, follow-up treatments, and doctor visits. I also felt they needed to know about the possibility of males getting breast cancer. I hoped they would share this information with their families and particularly with their male significant others.

As for attitude. I looked at this as "I have never had cancer and this will be a new and unique experience." I embraced it and was optimistic the entire way. I felt this was something where I would learn new things and engage with people I would otherwise not have contact with. I did a lot of self-evaluation and felt I had an expansive and rewarding life. Never did I feel sorry for myself, despondent, or fear the possibility of death. I had co-workers relate that I was the most optimistic person they had ever met that was dealing with cancer. And I was optimistic. I feel the optimism and positive perspective played a large part in my success with cancer."

According to the National Breast Cancer organization, (http://www.nationalbreastcancer.org/male-breast-cancer), breast cancer in men is usually detected as a hard lump underneath the nipple and areola. Men carry a higher mortality than women, primarily because awareness among men is less and they are not as likely to assume a lump is breast cancer, which can cause a delay in seeking treatment. So, please share this with as many people as you can and let's bring awareness to men too!

Printed in the United States
By Bookmasters